Global Issues in Property Law

By

John G. Sprankling
University of the Pacific,
McGeorge School of Law

Raymond R. Coletta
University of the Pacific,
McGeorge School of Law

M.C. Mirow
Florida International University
College of Law

AMERICAN CASEBOOK SERIES®

Mat #40445528

American Casebook Series and West Group are trademarks registered in the U.S. Patent and Trademark Office.

© 2006 Thomson/West
      610 Opperman Drive
      P.O. Box 64526
      St. Paul, MN 55164–0526
      1–800–328–9352

Printed in the United States of America

ISBN–13: 978–0–314–16729–3
ISBN–10: 0–314–16729–3

TEXT IS PRINTED ON 10% POST
CONSUMER RECYCLED PAPER

To Gail, Tom, and Doug

J.G.S.

To my family, Mom, Itzibu, Sean, and Julian

R.R.C.

To my parents, Gregory and Shirley

M.C.M.

*

Preface

There is no more fascinating area for the study of global legal issues than property law. Property law reflects the choices that each culture makes about how to allocate its resources. Accordingly, its development is a product of—and a catalyst for—the economic, political, and social forces that shape a society. Despite the extraordinary range of property rules found in different cultures, they tend to share a common core. Thus, a global perspective on property law illuminates both our similarities and our differences.

The standard, first-year law school course on property traditionally focuses on domestic law, primarily on state law. We believe that the study of comparative, transnational, and international law principles significantly enhances the course. So what should you expect from this book? First, we hope that it will provide new perspectives on domestic property law, which will help you understand the assumptions and limitations inherent in our own system. Different cultures often employ different approaches to common problems. Thus, learning about the property law of other nations helps us realize that our own system was not predestined or inevitable, but rather that it stems from rational choice. In turn, this allows us to evaluate our system in light of other models.

Second, this book will help to prepare you for the practice of law in the twenty-first century. Today lawyers are literally faced with a new world of practice, because legal problems cross national borders. Clients come from all parts of the globe—and legal challenges follow them. International trade, the internet, and global responses to terrorism and human rights violations, to name but a few influences, have reshaped the law. International law increasingly affects domestic property law. For example, in many regions, the right to property is now seen as a human right, which may be protected under international law. Similarly, even the most mundane transaction or dispute may have an international or transnational component; thus, a basic understanding of foreign legal systems and comparative law is a necessary tool for the modern lawyer.

This book, like the others in the Global Issues Series, reflects the view that Supreme Court Justice Stephen G. Breyer has expressed so eloquently: "This world we live in is a world where it is out of date to teach foreign law in a course called Foreign Law." We believe that law schools have a responsibility to introduce comparative, transnational, and international law principles in all key domestic courses. Toward that end, this book can be used as a supplement with any property casebook. Because the chapters are designed to stand on their own, they may be used in any order or in any combination. Our goal is to provide interesting and accessible materials that can be incorporated, in whole or in part, into any property course.

All of us would like to thank Thomson West—and particularly Louis Higgins—for sharing our vision that the Global Issues Series will make an important contribution to legal education. We wish to thank Frank Gevurtz, the overall series editor, who envisioned the series (and then made it a reality), and also Thom Main, whose pioneering work in writing the first book in the series made our task much easier. Finally, we would also like to thank Duncan Hollis, Errol Meidinger, and Patrick Randolph; this book benefited from insights that each of them offered in Summer, 2005 at the Globalizing the Law School Curriculum Workshop, sponsored by Pacific McGeorge, at Lake Tahoe, California.

John Sprankling and Raymond Coletta thank Pacific McGeorge Dean Elizabeth Rindskopf Parker and Associate Dean Christine Manolakas for their inspiration and support; colleagues Kojo Yelpaala and Samuel Manteaw for their insights into African legal principles, and John Sims for sharing his expertise in human rights law; and the Reference Librarians of the Gordon D. Schaber Law Library, especially Paul Howard, for providing needed research support.

John Sprankling thanks his co-authors for their creativity, collegiality, and patience. As always, his wife Gail Heckemeyer provided loving encouragement and careful proofreading.

Raymond Coletta would like to thank his co-authors for their intellectual insights, quiet patience, and wonderful collaboration, and Zebulon Young for providing excellent research assistance. He would be severely remiss not to acknowledge the extraordinary organizational and editing work done by co-author John Sprankling.

M.C. Mirow thanks his co-authors for making the collaborative process enjoyable and intellectually rewarding. Céline Abramschmitt and Germán Morales contributed significantly in both substance and style. Mirow's family, Angela, Camila, and Andrea, as always, provided constant, patient support.

As authors, we own any errors in the text, at least until someone with better title comes along.

JOHN G. SPRANKLING
RAYMOND R. COLETTA
M.C. MIROW

June, 2006

Acknowledgments

We gratefully acknowledge receiving permission to reprint the following materials:

Charles Aubry & Charles Rau, Droit Civil Français, Volume II (Paul Esmein, ed., 7th ed., 1961) (Louisiana State Law Institute, trans., St. Paul, West Publishing, 1966).

Countryside and Rights of Way Act, 2000, c. 37 (Eng.). © Crown Copyright 2000.

Debate in the House of Commons, March 26, 1999, 328 Parl. Deb., H.C. (6th ser.) (1999). Parliamentary material is reproduced with the permission of HMSO on behalf of Parliament.

Debate in the House of Lords, May 19, 1999, 601 Parl. Deb., H.L. (5th ser.) (1999). Parliamentary material is reproduced with the permission of HMSO on behalf of Parliament.

Hernando de Soto, The Mystery of Capital (Perseus Books Group, 2001). Copyright © 2001 by Hernando de Soto. Reprinted by permission of Basic Books, a member of Perseus Books, L.L.C.

Daniel Fitzpatrick, Disputes and Pluralism in Modern Indonesian Land Law, 22 Yale J. Int'l L. 171 (1997).

Alejandro M. Garro, Chapter 8: Recordation of Interests in Land, in International Encyclopedia of Comparative Law, Volume VI, Property and Trust (Athanassios N. Yiannopoulos, ed., 2004).

Kenneth L. Karst, Rights in Land and Housing in an Informal Legal System: The Barrios of Caracas, 19 Am. J. Comp. L. 550 (1971).

Deborah Kenn, One Nation's Dream, Another's Reality: Housing Justice in Sweden, 22 Brooklyn J. Int'l L. 63 (1996).

Winter King, Illegal Settlements and the Impact of Titling Programs, 44 Harv. Int'l L.J. 433 (2003) © (2003) by the President and Fellows of Harvard College and the Harvard International Law Journal.

Land Registry, United Kingdom, The Strategy for the Implementation of E-Conveyancing in England and Wales, October 2005. Produced by Land Registry and available from its website www.landregistry.gov.uk. © Crown copyright material is reproduced with the permission of Land Registry.

Matthew A. Light, Different Ideas of the City: Origins of Metropolitan Land-Use Regimes in the United States, Germany, and Switzerland, 24 Yale J. Int'l L. 577 (1999).

Daniel B. Magraw, International Land-Use Law, 87 Am. Soc'y Int'l L. Proc. 488 (1993). Reproduced with permission from © The American Society of International Law.

Ugo Mattei, Basic Principles of Property Law: A Comparative Legal and Economic Introduction. Copyright © 2000 by Ugo Mattei. Reproduced with permission of Greenwood Publishing Group, Inc., Westport, CT.

Roy H. May, The Poor of Land: A Christian Case for Land Reform (Maryknoll, New York: Orbis Books, 1991).

John Henry Merryman, Ownership and Estate (Variations on a Theme by Lawson), 48 Tul. L. Rev. 916 (1974). Reprinted with the permission of the Tulane Law Review, which holds the copyright.

Bernard Rudden, Economic Theory v. Property Law: The *Numerus Clausus* Problem, in Oxford Essays in Jurisprudence, Third Series (John Eekelaar & John Bell, eds., Clarendon Press, Oxford, 1987).

Bea Verschraegen, The Right to Private Life and Family Life, the Right to Marry and to Found a Family, and the Prohibition of Discrimination, in Legal Recognition of Same-Sex Couples in Europe (Katharina Boele-Woelki & Angelika Fuchs, eds., 2003).

Hans Ytterberg, All Human Beings Are Equal, But Are Some More Equal Than Others—Equality in Dignity Without Equality in Rights?, in Legal Recognition of Same-Sex Couples in Europe (Katharina Boele-Woelki & Angelika Fuchs, eds., 2003).

Global Issues Series

Series Editor, Franklin A. Gevurtz

Available for Fall 2006 Classes

Global Issues in Civil Procedure by Thomas Main, University of
the Pacific, McGeorge School of Law
ISBN 0–314–15978–9

Global Issues in Corporate Law by Franklin A. Gevurtz, University of the Pacific, McGeorge School of Law
ISBN 0–314–15977–0

Global Issues in Property Law by John G. Sprankling, University of the Pacific, McGeorge School of Law, Raymond R. Coletta, University of the Pacific, McGeorge School of Law, and M.C. Mirow,
Florida International University College of Law
ISBN 0–314–16729–3

For Spring 2007 adoption, we also expect to have titles available in
Contracts, Criminal Law, Labor Law, and Professional Responsibility.

*

Summary of Contents

Table of Contents

*

Table of Cases

The principal cases are in bold type. Cases cited or discussed in the text are roman type. References are to pages. Cases cited in principal cases and within other quoted materials are not included.

*

xix

Global Issues in Property Law

*

Chapter 1

DEFINING "PROPERTY"

How do we define "property"? There is no internationally-accepted definition of the term. It may be difficult to define "property" even under the domestic law of a particular country. In fact, most of your course in property is devoted to defining what "property" means in the United States.

In the United States, we broadly define "property" as legally-enforceable rights among people that relate to "things." The particular "thing" might be land, or a tangible object (such as this book), or an intangible item (such as the goodwill of a business). Thus, to understand the meaning of "property" in our system we ask two questions: (1) what rights are legally-protected? and (2) what are the "things" that one can hold legally-protected rights in? Of course, this two-step approach is not an international standard. Legal scholars in many nations would approach the definition of "property" from quite different perspectives, as the materials below reflect. But at least it provides a place to begin.

The definitions of property used in different nations—and in international law as well—often share a common core. Yet they also differ substantially in some respects. The goal of this chapter is to start you thinking about *why* different systems define property differently. This process, in turn, will help you to understand what property means in the United States.

This book will introduce you to property law systems in Africa, Asia, Europe, and the Americas. Most of these systems have been influenced by either the *civil law* or *common law* traditions. The civil law tradition traces its lineage back to ancient Rome, but was revitalized after the French Revolution by the French Civil Code of 1804. The civil law approach is followed in European nations (for example, France, Germany, Italy, and Spain); it has also heavily influenced former European colonies (including most nations in

1

South America and many in Africa). In addition, nations that sought to modernize their legal systems over the last two centuries (for example, Japan, Russia, and Vietnam) often adopted the civil law approach. The common law approach, in contrast, is followed in the United Kingdom and in former British colonies, including Australia, Canada, India, and the United States.

A. PROPERTY AS LEGALLY–ENFORCEABLE RIGHTS

Property in the United States is classically viewed as a "bundle of rights." The rights in this bundle include, at a minimum: (a) the right to possess and use; (b) the right to exclude others; and (c) the right to transfer. As noted below, civil law nations follow a somewhat different approach.

John Henry Merryman
Ownership and Estate (Variations on a Theme by Lawson)

48 Tul. L. Rev. 916, 918, 924–25, 927–28 (1974)

. . . Productive comparative study of the land law in civil and common law jurisdictions is difficult—perhaps impossible—without some understanding of a fundamental difference that can be summarized by saying that the former is a law of ownership and the latter is one of estate. While it is probably true that a few lawyers in either system know that there is a difference and that it is important, few have gone much beyond this general impression. In this essay, I attempt to provide something more substantial by discussing the differences between ownership and estate in the two systems and, more specifically, in the land law of Italy and that of a more or less typical common law jurisdiction in the United States. Italian property law is not exactly like that of any other civil law nation, but it probably comes as close to a "typical" civil law property system as any other and closer than most. Much of what is said here is accordingly applicable to the land law in other West European nations and throughout Latin America.

. . . Ownership is, as concepts go, a very powerful one, and those who employ it pay its price. The land law of Italy and other civil law nations, based firmly on Roman law, is a law of individual ownership. . . . [It] strongly resists fragmentation. To say that I own a thing is to imply that you do not, for if it is yours how can it be mine? Such thinking thus tends to eliminate all intermediate possibilities between ownership and non-ownership. Consequently, when it becomes desirable to equate power over land with more than one person it seems preferable to do so by a device which, at least apparently, avoids dividing ownership. In every transaction ownership must be transferred *in toto* or not at all.

This, although simplified, gives some of the flavor of ownership in the Italian land law. Although its non-legal composition may vary from time to time with social and economic change, legal ownership remains exclusive, single, and indivisible. Only one person can own the same thing at the same time. But, since the requirements of society are such that power over land must frequently be divided between individuals, it becomes necessary to rationalize the dictates of theory and the requirements of practice. . . .

The inconsistency between ownership and fragmentation can, of course, be exaggerated. Even in the civil law, land can be "owned" simultaneously by two or more persons *in comune*, a form of co-ownership much like our tenancy in common. But a functional distinction between beneficial and security title, or between legal and equitable title, or a temporal division into present and future estates, simply does not exist. Ownership is, in theory, invisible in function and time. . . .

The basic difference between Romanic ownership and the Anglo–American "estate" or "interest" in land can be illustrated by a simple metaphor. Romanic ownership can be thought of as a box, with the word "ownership" written on it. Whoever has the box is the "owner." In the case of complete, unencumbered ownership, the box contains certain rights, including that of use and occupancy, that to the fruits or income, and the power of alienation. The owner can, however, open the box and remove one or more such rights and transfer them to others. But, as long as he keeps the box, he still has the ownership, even if the box is empty. The contrast with the Anglo–American law of property is simple. There is no box. There are merely various sets of legal interests. One who has the fee simple absolute has the largest possible bundle of such sets of legal interests. When he conveys one or more of them to another person, a part of his bundle is gone.

This basic difference has several possible theoretical consequences. First, tenure seems to be a more flexible concept than ownership. Consequently, it might be expected that the number and variety of institutionalized interests in land will be greater in a tenure than in an ownership property system. . . .

The much greater variety of permissible future interests (vested and contingent remainders, executory interests, powers of appointment, reversions, rights of entry, possibilities of reverter) in the common law than in the civil law (where they really do not exist) supports this prediction. It is further supported by the existence of the trust and the concept of separate legal and equitable interests and by the distinction between security interests and beneficial interests in land, both found in the common law but not in the civil law. . . .

Civil Code of Vietnam

Article 173: Ownership rights comprise the right to possession, the right to use and the right to disposal with respect to the property of the owner in accordance with the provisions of law. An owner may be an individual, a legal person or another entity having all three rights which are the right to possession, the right to use and the right to disposal of the property. . . .

Article 189: The right to possession is the right of an owner to keep and manage by himself/herself the property under his/her ownership. . . .

Article 198: The right to use is the right of an owner to exploit the utility and to enjoy the fruits and profits from the property. . . .

Article 201: The right to disposal is the right of an owner to transfer his/her ownership right over a property to another person or persons or to renounce such ownership right. . . .

Article 222: . . . An individual has the right to possession, use and disposal of his/her privately-owned property for the purpose of serving the needs of daily life and consumption, or production and business and other purposes in accordance with the provisions of law. . . .

Notes

1.   What are the rights "in the box" that constitute ownership of land in Italy? How do these rights compare to the "ownership rights" set forth in Article 173 of the Civil Code of Vietnam? To our definition of the "bundle of rights" that constitute property in the United States?

2.   The extent to which a particular property right is recognized varies among nations. For instance, the Constitution of the Republic of Cuba provides that "the state recognizes the rights of small farmers to legal ownership of their lands" but permits them to transfer title only to the national government, an agricultural cooperative, or another small farmer (Article 19). Similarly, lands owned by small farmers may be inherited only by "those heirs who work the land" (Article 24). What social policy do these limitations serve?

3.   Article 173 of the Civil Code of Vietnam defines an "owner" as a person who has "all three rights." How is this similar to, or different from, the concept of "absolute ownership" of land in Italy? These concepts are discussed in more detail in Chapter 3.

B. RIGHTS IN WHAT?

A second question is: what are the "things" that one may hold property rights in? The answer to this question varies—sometimes dramatically—from nation to nation.

1. Common Heritage Regions

International law sometimes limits the scope of private property rights. In particular, some regions of the world (and the universe) are increasingly viewed as the "common heritage" of all humans, and thus not subject to private property rights. For example, can someone own the moon?

AGREEMENT GOVERNING THE ACTIVITIES OF STATES ON THE MOON AND OTHER CELESTIAL BODIES

(1979)

Article 11:

1.   The Moon and its natural resources are the common heritage of all mankind....

3.   Neither the surface nor the subsurface of the Moon, nor any part thereof or natural resources in place, shall become the property of any State, international intergovernmental or nongovernmental organization, national organization or non-governmental entity or of any natural person. The placement of personnel, space vehicles, equipment, facilities, stations and installations on or below the surface of the Moon, including structures connected with its surface or subsurface, shall not create a right of ownership over the surface or the subsurface of the Moon or any areas thereof. ...

Notes

1.   Only 11 nations have signed and ratified the "Moon Treaty." Significantly, China, Russia, and the United States have refused to sign the treaty. Does this mean that we should view the moon as potential private property? Using the internet, you will quickly discover many companies that are eager to sell land on the moon. Suppose you purchased title to moon land from one of these companies. Exactly what would you own?

2.   The 1967 Treaty on Principles Governing the Activities of States in the Exploration and Use of Outer Space, Including the Moon and Other Celestial Bodies, provides that "[o]uter space, including the moon and other celestial bodies, is not subject to national appropriation by claim of sovereignty, by means of use or occupation, or by any other

means" (Article II). However, it says nothing about private property rights. This treaty has been ratified by the United States and over 60 other nations.

3.   Most nations have ratified the United Nations Convention on the Law of the Sea; the United States is a prominent exception. The Convention provides, in part, that the "sea-bed and ocean floor and subsoil thereof beyond the limits of national jurisdiction" are the "common heritage of mankind," and thus cannot be claimed as private property (Articles 1 and 136). Should there be other regions that cannot be the subject of private property rights?

2. *Land*

In a sense, the most basic form of property consists of rights in land. But some nations do not recognize this form of property. And even in the vast majority of nations that allow property rights in land, the scope of those rights can vary widely.

Civil Code of Vietnam

Article 205: The land, mountains and forests, rivers and lakes, water sources, natural resources under ground, resources from the sea, continental shelf and airspace, and the capital and property invested by the State in enterprises and facilities in the branches and fields of economy, culture, social welfare, sciences, technology, foreign affairs, and national defense and security, and other property stipulated by law to be of the State, come under ownership of the entire people. . . .

Article 221: (1) Legitimate income, savings, residential houses, means of daily life, means of production, capital, fruits and other legitimate properties of an individual are privately-owned properties. Legitimate privately-owned properties shall not be restricted in quantity and value. (2) An individual cannot be the owner of a property which cannot be privately owned under law.

Basic Law of Government, Kingdom of Saudi Arabia

Article 14: All God's bestowed wealth, be it under the ground, on the surface or in national territorial waters, in the land or maritime domains under the state's control, are the property of the state as defined by law. . . .

John Henry Merryman
Ownership and Estate (Variations on a Theme by Lawson)

48 Tul. L. Rev. 916, 935–37 (1974)

It is an interesting historical paradox that the lease of land...has become the only surviving example of the tenurial relationship between lord and tenant in our land law ...[T]he lease...retains a part of its feudal character in our law, and the common term applied to the relationship—"landlord and tenant"—is still to some extent descriptive. The lease, even when it pertains to commercial premises in an urban area, is still considered to be an instrument of conveyance of an estate in the land, like the deed. It is not a contract. ... The law governing leases is a part of the law of property, and in this way it was, by definition, excluded from the great creative development of commercial law in England.

In Italian law, the lease is a contract. ... [T]ransactions that have purposes analogous to our leases of land create only personal rights in the lessee. No real rights—no part of the ownership of the land—are conveyed to him. The law governing leases is found in that part of the Civil Code dealing with obligations, rather than in the part dealing with property. As a consequence, the two systems start with quite different premises. The Italian law adopts contract principles and modifies them when necessary in order to deal appropriately with the peculiar nature and subject-matter of the lease. The common law struggles to overcome the remaining traces of feudalism and to bring contract principles to bear on a property transaction that frequently is primarily commercial in purpose and significance.

Notes

1. Land cannot be privately owned in Vietnam. Thus, a person may own her own house, but not the land that lies beneath it. Why? What impact does state ownership of land have on a nation's economic, social, and cultural life?

2. In Saudi Arabia, mineral rights—including the right to oil—are the property of the government. Many other oil-producing nations follow the same approach. However, in the United States mineral rights in privately-owned land are seen as private property. Which approach is better and why?

3. The excerpt from Professor Merryman's article points out that the lease is viewed as a form of contract in Italy, not the conveyance of an interest in land. Modern law in the United States now seems to view the lease as a hybrid—partly governed by property law, and partly by contract law. Does it matter whether a lease is considered a contract or a conveyance?

3. *Intangibles*

Almost all nations recognize that property rights can exist in intangibles. For instance, property rights in copyrights, patents, trademarks, and other forms of intellectual property are usually recognized. Indeed, the nature and scope of these rights is increasingly affected by international law. However, nations differ on whether property rights can be created in other intangibles.

VAN MARLE AND OTHERS v. THE NETHERLANDS

European Court of Human Rights
8 Eur. H.R. Rep. 483, 490–91 (1986)

RYSSDAL, GANSHOF VAN DER MEERSCH, CREMONA, WIARDA, VILHJÁLMSSON, BINDSCHEDLER–ROBERT, LAGERGREN, GÖLCÜKLÜ, MATSCHER, PINHEIRO FARINHA, PETTITI, WALSH, EVANS, MACDONALD, RUSSO, BERNHARDT, GERSING, and SPIELMANN, JUDGES.

[Applicants Van Marle and others worked as accountants for some years. The Netherlands then adopted a new statute, which provided that only a person meeting certain minimum professional qualifications could use the title "accountant." The applicants, who did not meet these standards, claimed that the statute violated their right to property under the European Convention for the Protection of Human Rights and Fundamental Freedoms; they brought suit in the European Court of Human Rights. Part of the Court's opinion is excerpted below, with the original paragraph numbers.]

39. ...[Van Marle and others] alleged that, as a result of the Board of Appeal's decisions, their income and the value of the goodwill of their accountancy practices had diminished. They maintained that they had thereby been subjected to an interference with the exercise of their right to the peaceful enjoyment of their possessions and to a partial deprivation thereof without compensation.

40. The Government, on the other hand, contended that the applicants had no "acquired right" to the use of the title "accountant" before the entry into force of the legislation regulating the use of that title. They contended that until then there was no legally recognised and protected right, but only a freedom to use the title. ... The Government also pointed out that as a matter of Netherlands law there was no such thing as a "right to goodwill" which could be regarded as property for the purposes of the [Convention].
. . .

41. The Court agrees...that the right relied upon by the applicants may be likened to the right of property embodied in [the Convention]: by dint of their own work, the applicants had built up

a clientele; this had in many respects the nature of a private right and constituted an asset, and, hence, a possession within the meaning of [the Convention]. . . .

METHANEX CORPORATION v. UNITED STATES

International Arbitration Tribunal
Final Award of the Tribunal on Jurisdiction and Merits
44 I.L.M 1345, 1372, 1457 (2005)

ROWLEY, REISMAN, and VEEDER, ARBITRATORS.

[Methanex Corporation, a Canadian company, was the world's largest producer of the chemical substance called methanol. Methanol was the key ingredient in MTBE, a gasoline additive that reduced air pollution. MTBE was added to gasoline sold in California until 1999, when Governor Gray Davis prohibited its use, due to concern that gasoline containing MTBE might leak from storage tanks and contaminate groundwater, posing a threat to public health and the environment. Methanex was the largest supplier of the methanol that was used to make MTBE for the California market. Methanex claimed that the California ban was "tantamount to expropriation" of its market share for the sale of methanol, in violation of the North American Free Trade Agreement (NAFTA). In this arbitration, it sought $970,000,000 in compensatory damages. Methanex lost on the merits of its claim, but the tribunal agreed that a "market share" was a form of property protected under NAFTA.]

. . .Methanex claims (inter alia) that the US measures have deprived and will continue to deprive Methanex and Methanex–US of a substantial portion of their customer base, goodwill and market for methanol in California. Methanex claims that California has essentially taken part of the US business of Methanex and Methanex–US and handed it directly to its competitor, the US ethanol industry. . . .

. . .Methanex claims that it lost customer base, goodwill and market share. The USA contends that none of these qualify as investments under Article 1139 [of NAFTA] and hence are not compensable.

The USA is correct that Article 1139 does not mention the items claimed by Methanex. But in *Pope & Talbot Inc. v. Canada*, the tribunal held that "the Investor's access to the U.S. market is a property interest subject to protection under Article 1110." Certainly, the restrictive notion of property as a material "thing" is obsolete and has ceded its place to a contemporary conception which includes managerial control over components of a process that is wealth producing. In the view of the Tribunal, items such as goodwill and market share may, as Professor White wrote, "constitute . . . an element of the value of an enterprise and as such may have been covered by some of the compensation elements." . . .

Notes

1. A property right to practice a profession is more likely to be recognized in Europe than in the United States. Exactly what did the court decide in *Van Marle*? Did it hold that the right to use a professional title is a property right?

2. In the United States, the dominant view is that property rights cannot exist in the "market share" of a particular business, because such an interest is too tenuous. Does the *Methanex* decision mean that the scope of property rights in the United States is broader for a Canadian corporation under NAFTA than for a U.S. corporation under domestic law? More broadly, what does it mean to say that a property right exists in "managerial control over components of a process that is wealth producing"? What might be property under this definition?

Chapter 2

PROPERTY AS A HUMAN RIGHT

A. HUMAN RIGHTS AND PROPERTY

Modern international law increasingly recognizes that individuals should enjoy certain basic "human rights." Although the lineage of this movement can be traced to natural law concepts, it is best understood as a response to the atrocities committed in Nazi Germany. In the post-World War II era, nations around the world acknowledged that certain rights—such as the right to be free from torture—were so fundamental that they should be protected by the international community. Thus, the 1945 United Nations Charter— a treaty that now binds over 190 nations—provides that the U.N. should promote "universal respect for, and observance of, human rights and fundamental freedoms" (U.N. Charter, Article 55). In 1948, the U.N. General Assembly adopted the Universal Declaration of Human Rights, and other human rights agreements soon followed.

The right to own property is broadly guaranteed by the Universal Declaration, and by regional human rights agreements adopted in Africa, the Americas, and Europe. But do these provisions create binding obligations or are they merely aspirational statements? The answer to this question remains somewhat uneven. The Universal Declaration was adopted by resolution, without the binding force of a treaty. Thus, initially it was seen as an aspirational document, whose lofty sentiments would be transformed into obligations through later treaties. However, progress toward this goal was slow during the Cold War era. In particular, the Soviet bloc firmly opposed creating an enforceable right to private property.

Many European nations joined together in 1953 to adopt the Convention for the Protection of Human Rights and Fundamental Freedoms, commonly called the "European Convention on Human Rights." A right to property was added to the Convention through Protocol 1, effective in 1954. Today the Convention is the most effective human rights treaty in the world. In over 40 European nations, an individual may invoke the right to property established by the Convention in a domestic court and, if unsatisfied with the outcome, may appeal to the European Court of Human Rights. Thus, the European Court is developing and enforcing an international jurisprudence that defines the scope of the right to property.

Outside of the European Convention on Human Rights, the enforceability of a human right to property is less certain. Although some portions of the Universal Declaration are accepted as creating legal obligations—whether as interpretations of the human rights obligations in the U.N. Charter or as customary international law—this process has not yet encompassed the right to property. However, based on the progress made under the European Convention and, to some extent, under human rights agreements in the Americas, there is a clear trend toward recognizing an internationally-enforceable right to property.

B.   INTERNATIONAL HUMAN RIGHTS AGREEMENTS

UNIVERSAL DECLARATION OF HUMAN RIGHTS
(1948)

Article 17:

(1) Everyone has the right to own property alone as well as in association with others.

(2) No one shall be arbitrarily deprived of his property.

AMERICAN DECLARATION OF THE RIGHTS AND DUTIES OF MAN
(1948)

Article XXIII: Every person has a right to own such private property as meets the essential needs of decent living and helps to maintain the dignity of the individual and of the home.

CONVENTION FOR THE PROTECTION OF HUMAN RIGHTS AND FUNDAMENTAL FREEDOMS, PROTOCOL 1
(1954)

Article 1—Protection of property

Every natural or legal person is entitled to the peaceful enjoyment of his possessions. No one shall be deprived of his possessions except in the public interest and subject to the conditions provided for by law and by the general principles of international law.

The preceding provisions shall not, however, in any way impair the right of a State to enforce such laws as it deems necessary to control the use of property in accordance with the general interest or to secure the payment of taxes or other contributions or penalties.

AMERICAN CONVENTION ON HUMAN RIGHTS

(1978)

Article 21. Right to Property

1. Everyone has the right to the use and enjoyment of his property. The law may subordinate such use and enjoyment to the interest of society.

2. No one shall be deprived of his property except upon payment of just compensation, for reasons of public utility or social interest, and in the cases and according to the forms established by law. . . .

AFRICAN CHARTER ON HUMAN AND PEOPLES' RIGHTS

(1981)

Article 14: The right to property shall be guaranteed. It may only be encroached upon in the interest of public need or in the general interest of the community and in accordance with the provisions of appropriate laws.

Notes

1. Some commentators suggest that the Universal Declaration of Human Rights is as important to the world as the Magna Carta was to England or the Declaration of Independence was to the United States. What are the implications of recognizing a human right to property? How would this affect the conduct of a sovereign nation within its borders?

2. After long negotiations, two treaties were adopted to implement the aspirational goals of the Universal Declaration: the Interna-

tional Covenant on Economic, Social and Cultural Rights and the International Covenant on Civil and Political Rights. The Covenants came into force in 1976, and now bind over 140 nations. However, due to Soviet bloc opposition, neither covenant includes the right to property. Should the United States propose a new treaty to create an internationally-enforceable right to property?

C. A HUMAN RIGHT TO ABORIGINAL LAND OWNERSHIP

Do aboriginal peoples have a human right to ownership of the lands their ancestors traditionally occupied? This is one of the concrete issues that has surfaced in the evolving jurisprudence of the right to property.

The two illustrative decisions below arise under the American Declaration of the Rights and Duties of Man (1948) and the later American Convention on Human Rights (1978), under the framework of the Organization of American States (OAS). The OAS Charter—a treaty binding the United States and most nations in the Americas—proclaims the importance of protecting "the fundamental rights of the individual." The American Declaration was initially adopted as a non-binding OAS resolution. However, over time it has been accepted as the authoritative interpretation of the "fundamental rights" guaranteed by the OAS Charter. Disputes arising under the American Declaration are heard by the Inter–American Commission on Human Rights, which consists of seven members elected by OAS nations. The American Convention, in contrast, is a treaty which both creates enforceable human rights obligations and establishes a special court—the Inter–American Court of Human Rights—to adjudicate human rights disputes; only the Commission can bring an action in this Court. The United States is not a party to the American Convention; President Carter signed the Convention, but it was not ratified by the Senate.

THE MAYAGNA (SUMO) AWAS TINGNI COMMUNITY v. NICARAGUA

Inter–American Court of Human Rights
Inter–Am. Ct. H.R. (Ser. C) No. 79 (2001)

CANCADO, PACHECO–GÓMEZ, SALGADO–PESANTES, JACKMAN, ABREU–BURELLI, GARCIA–RAMÍREZ, ROUX–RENGIFO, and ARGUELLO, JUDGES.

[The Mayagna (Sumo) Awas Tingi Community is a group of about 650 indigenous people living in Nicaragua near the Atlantic Coast. Members of the community subsist on communal farming, hunting, fishing, and gathering. The community claimed ownership of over 300 square miles of undeveloped, tropical forest lands, which had been traditionally occupied by its ancestors. The government of Nicaragua recognized—in theory—that aboriginal peoples had rights in the land they occupied, and it had established a mechanism to formalize their land titles; in practice, however, these rights were largely ignored. Over many years, despite repeated requests, no indigenous communities had received deeds confirming ownership of their lands. In 1996, a government agency granted a 30–year logging concession over most of the community's lands to a Korean timber corporation. Concerned that its forests would be cut, the community challenged the legality of the logging concession through suit in Nicaraguan courts, without success. It then filed a petition with the Inter–American Commission on Human Rights which, in turn, brought an action against Nicaragua in the Inter–American Court of Human Rights under the American Convention. An excerpt from the Court's decision, with the original paragraph numbers, is set forth below.]

. . .

143.   Article 21 of the American Convention recognizes the right to private property. In this regard, it establishes: a) that "[e]veryone has the right to the use and enjoyment of his property"; b) that such use and enjoyment can be subordinate, according to a legal mandate, to "social interest"; c) that a person may be deprived of his or her property for reasons of "public utility or social interest, and in the cases and according to the forms established by law"; and d) that when so deprived, a just compensation must be paid.

144.   "Property" can be defined as those material things which can be possessed, as well as any right which may be part of a person's patrimony; that concept includes all moveables and immoveables, corporeal and incorporeal elements and any other intangible object capable of having value. . . .

146.   The terms of an international human rights treaty have an autonomous meaning, for which reason they cannot be made equivalent to the meaning given to them in domestic law. Furthermore, such human rights treaties are live instruments whose interpretation must adapt to the evolution of the times and, specifically, to current living conditions.

147.   Article 29(b) of the Convention, in turn, establishes that no provision may be interpreted as "restricting the enjoyment or exercise of any right or freedom recognized by virtue of the laws of any State Party or by virtue of another convention to which one of the said states is a party."

148.   Through an evolutionary interpretation of international instruments for the protection of human rights, taking into account applicable norms of interpretation and pursuant to article 29(b) of the Convention—which precludes a restrictive interpretation of

rights—, it is the opinion of this Court that article 21 of the Convention protects the right to property in a sense which includes, among others, the rights of the members of indigenous communities within the framework of communal property, which is also recognized by the Constitution of Nicaragua.

149. Given the characteristics of the instant case, some specifications are required on the concept of property in indigenous communities. Among indigenous peoples there is a communitarian tradition regarding a communal form of collective property of the land, in the sense that ownership of the land is not centered on an individual but rather on the group and its community. Indigenous groups, by the fact of their very existence, have the right to live freely in their own territory; the close ties of indigenous peoples with the land must be recognized and understood as the fundamental basis of their cultures, their spiritual life, their integrity, and their economic survival. For indigenous communities, relations to the land are not merely a matter of possession and production but a material and spiritual element which they must fully enjoy, even to preserve their cultural legacy and transmit it to future generations. . . .

151. Indigenous peoples' customary law must be especially taken into account for the purpose of this analysis. As a result of customary practices, possession of the land should suffice for indigenous communities lacking real title to property of the land to obtain official recognition of that property, and for consequent registration.

152. As has been pointed out, Nicaragua recognizes communal property of indigenous peoples, but has not regulated the specific procedure to materialize that recognition, and therefore no such title deeds have been granted since 1990. Furthermore, in the instant case the State has not objected to the claim of the Awas Tingni Community to be declared owner, even though the extent of the area claimed is disputed.

153. It is the opinion of the Court that, pursuant to article 5 of the Constitution of Nicaragua, the members of the Awas Tingni Community have a communal right to the lands they currently inhabit, without detriment to the rights of other indigenous communities... Based on this understanding, the Court considers that the members of the Awas Tingni have the right that the State a) carry out the delimitation, demarcation, and titling of the territory belonging to the Community; and b) abstain from carrying out, until that delimitation, demarcation, and titling have been done, actions that might lead the agents of the State itself, or third parties acting with its acquiescence or its tolerance, to affect the existence, value, use or enjoyment of the property located in the

geographical area where the members of the Community live and carry out their activities.... [T]he Court believes that, in light of article 21 of the Convention, the State has violated the right of the members of the Mayagna Awas Tingni Community to the use and enjoyment of their property, and that it has granted concessions to third parties to utilize the property and resources located in an area which could correspond, fully or in part, to the lands which must be delimited, demarcated, and titled....

DANN v. UNITED STATES

Inter–American Commission on Human Rights
Case No. 11.140, Inter–Am. C.H.R., Report No. 75/02 (2002)

MENDÉZ, ALTOLAGUIRRE, ZALAQUETT, VALLEJO, ROBERTS and VILLARÁN, COMMISSIONERS.

[In 1951, the Shoshone Tribe sought compensation before the United States Indian Claims Commission for the tribe's loss of title to lands located in California, Colorado, Idaho, Nevada, Utah, and Wyoming. In 1962, that commission ruled that the aboriginal title of the Western Shoshone had been extinguished in the nineteenth century; it later awarded the tribe $26,000,000 in compensation for these lands. Before this ruling became final, Carrie and Mary Dann and other members of the Western Shoshone unsuccessfully attempted to intervene in the proceedings to exclude certain lands in Nevada which they claimed had never been taken. In 1974, the United States brought a trespass action against the Danns, alleging that they were illegally grazing livestock on public lands in Nevada without a permit. In defense, the Danns asserted that the Western Shoshone still held aboriginal title to the land. After extensive litigation, the Supreme Court held in *United States v. Dann*, 470 U.S. 39 (1985) that the aboriginal title had been finally extinguished when the United States deposited the awarded funds into a trust account for the tribe. In 1993, the Danns filed a petition with the Inter–American Commission on Human Rights, asserting that the conduct of the United States violated their rights under the American Declaration.]

. . .

128. ...[T]he Commission and other international authorities have recognized...a particular connection between communities of indigenous peoples and the lands and resources that they have traditionally occupied and used, the preservation of which is fundamental to the effective realization of the human rights of indigenous peoples more generally and therefore warrants special measures of protection. The Commission has observed, for example, that continued utilization of traditional collective systems for the control and use of territory are in many instances essential to the

individual and collective well-being, and indeed the survival of, indigenous peoples and that control over the land refers both to its capacity for providing the resources which sustain life, and to the geographic space necessary for the cultural and social reproduction of the group. The Inter–American Court of Human Rights has similarly recognized that for indigenous communities the relation with the land is not merely a question of possession and production but has a material and spiritual element that must be fully enjoyed to preserve their cultural legacy and pass it on to future generations. . . .

130.   Of particular relevance to the present case, the Commission considers that general international legal principles applicable in the context of indigenous human rights include:

• the right of indigenous peoples to legal recognition of their varied and specific forms and modalities of their control, ownership, use and enjoyment of territories and property;

• the recognition of their property and ownership rights with respect to lands, territories and resources they have historically occupied; and

• where property and user rights of indigenous peoples arise from rights existing prior to the creation of a state, recognition by that state of the permanent and inalienable title of indigenous peoples relative thereto and to have such title changed only by mutual consent between the state and respective indigenous peoples when they have full knowledge and appreciation of the nature or attributes of such property. This also implies the right to fair compensation in the event that such property and user rights are irrevocably lost.

131.   Based on the foregoing analysis, the Commission is of the view that the provisions of the American Declaration should be interpreted and applied in the context of indigenous petitioners with due regard to the particular principles of international human rights law governing the individual and collective interests of indigenous peoples. Particularly pertinent provisions of the Declaration in this respect include Article II (the right to equality under the law), Article XVIII (the right to a fair trial), and Article XXIII (the right to property). As outlined above, this approach includes the taking of special measures to ensure recognition of the particular and collective interest that indigenous peoples have in the occupation and use of their traditional lands and resources and their right not to be deprived of this interest except with fully informed consent, under conditions of equality, and with fair compensation. . . .

140.   The Commission first considers that Articles XVIII and XXIII of the American Declaration specially oblige a member state to

ensure that any determination of the extent to which indigenous claimants maintain interests in the lands to which they have traditionally held title and have occupied and used is based upon a process of fully informed and mutual consent on the part of the indigenous community as a whole. This requires at a minimum that all of the members of the community are fully and accurately informed of the nature and consequences of the process and provided with an effective opportunity to participate individually or as collectives. In the case of the Danns, however, the record indicates that the land claim issue was pursued by one band of the Western Shoshone people with no apparent mandate from the other Western Shoshone bands or members. There is also no evidence on the record that appropriate consultations were held within the Western Shoshone at the time that certain significant determinations were made. This includes in particular the ICC's finding that the entirety of the Western Shoshone interest in their ancestral lands, which interests affect the Danns, was extinguished at some point in the past. . . .

142. The insufficiency of this process was augmented by the fact that, on the evidence, the issue of extinguishment was not litigated before or determined by the ICC, in that the ICC did not conduct an independent review of historical and other evidence to determine as a matter of fact whether the Western Shoshone properly claimed title to all or some of their traditional lands. Rather, the ICC determination was based upon an agreement between the State and the purported Western Shoshone representatives as to the extent and timing of the extinguishment. . . . [I]t cannot be said that the Danns' claims to property rights in the Western Shoshone ancestral lands were determined through an effective and fair process in compliance with the norms and principles under Articles XVIII and XXIII of the American Declaration. . . .

171. The Commission wishes to emphasize that it is not for this body in the circumstances of the present case to determine whether and to what extent the Danns may properly claim a subsisting right to property in the Western Shoshone ancestral lands. This issue involves complex issues of law and fact that are more appropriately left to the State for determination through those legal processes it may consider suitable for that purpose. These processes must, however, conform with the norms and principles under the American Declaration applicable to the determination of indigenous property rights as elucidated in this report. This requires in particular that the Danns be afforded resort to the courts for the protection of their property rights, in conditions of equality and in a manner that considers both the collective and individual nature of the property rights that the Danns may claim in the Western Shoshone ancestral lands. The process must also allow for the Danns' full and informed

participation in the determination of their claims to property rights in the Western Shoshone ancestral lands.

172. Based upon the foregoing analysis, the Commission hereby concludes that the State has failed to ensure the Danns' right to property under conditions of equality contrary to Articles II, XVIII, and XXIII of the American Declaration in connection with their claims to property rights in the Western Shoshone ancestral lands.

173. In accordance with the analysis and conclusions in the present report, the Inter–American Commission on Human Rights reiterates the following recommendations to the United States:

1. Provide Mary and Carrie Dann with an effective remedy, which includes adopting the legislative or other measures necessary to ensure respect for the Danns' right to property in accordance with Articles II, XVIII, and XXIII of the American Declaration in connection with their claims to property rights in the Western Shoshone ancestral lands.

2. Review its laws, procedures, and practices to ensure that the property rights of indigenous persons are determined in accordance with the rights established in the American Declaration. . . .

Notes

1. Does *Mayagna (Sumo) Awas Tingni Community* stand for the proposition that international human rights law will recognize that aboriginal peoples hold title to the lands they have traditionally occupied? If so, what are the implications of this approach? *See also Maya Indigenous Communities v. Belize*, Case No. 12.053, Inter–Amer. C.H.R., Report No. 40/04 (2004) (Commission report holding that Belize violated land title rights of Maya communities).

2. Exactly what does the Commission decide in *Dann*? Does it recognize the right of the United States to extinguish the Danns' title, assuming that an appropriate procedure is followed? What is the significance of Paragraph 140 of the decision, which requires the United States to use a "process of fully informed and mutual consent on the part of the indigenous community as a whole"? How might *Dann* affect the rights of other Native Americans in the United States? To date, the United States has refused to abide by the outcome in *Dann*. For additional information about this case, see Deborah Schaaf & Julie Fishel, Mary and Carrie Dann v. United States *at the Inter–American Commission on Human Rights: Victory for Indian Land Rights and the Environment*, 16 Tul. Envtl. L.J. 175 (2002).

3. Compare the approaches to aboriginal property rights taken in *Mayagna (Sumo) Awas Tingi Community* and *Dann*. How do they differ? Which approach do you favor?

4. Article 26 of the United Nations Draft Declaration on the Rights of Indigenous Peoples provides: "Indigenous peoples have the

right to own, develop, control, and use the lands and territories...which they traditionally owned or otherwise occupied. This includes the full recognition of their laws, traditions and customs, land-tenure systems and institutions for the development and management of resources, and the right to effective measures by States to prevent any interference with, alienation of or encroachment upon these rights."

5. In *Johnson v. M'Intosh*, 21 U.S. (8 Wheat.) 543 (1823), the United States Supreme Court ruled that the federal government held title to the lands occupied by Native Americans, subject only to their "right of occupancy." The Court explained that: "Conquest gives a title which the Courts of the conqueror cannot deny." *Id.* at 588. Contrast this approach with the holdings in *Mayagna (Sumo) Awas Tingni Community* and *Dann.*

6. Land title has traditionally been seen as a purely domestic matter—an area where international law could not intrude. As the Supreme Court commented in *Johnson v. M'Intosh, supra* at 572: "[T]itle to lands...must be admitted to depend entirely on the law of the nation in which they lie." Both *Mayagna (Sumo) Awas Tingni Community* and *Dann* were brought before international tribunals after the complaining parties had fully—but unsuccessfully—litigated their claims in the domestic court system. To what extent should international tribunals defer to land title decisions made by national courts?

7. What effect might Article XXIII of the American Declaration have on other property law issues that arise in the United States? For instance, would it provide the homeless residents of New York City with a right to decent housing? Could an impoverished tenant in California use the rule as a defense to an eviction for failure to pay rent?

Chapter 3

FEE SIMPLE ABSOLUTE

A. THE FEE SIMPLE ABSOLUTE IN HISTORY

Fee simple absolute is the most complete ownership possible of real property in the common law. It is important to understand that this estate was the product of the unique political, economic, and social forces that prevailed in England during the centuries following the Norman Conquest of 1066. Fee simple absolute evolved through case law in a legal system that was relatively isolated from outside influences, despite its proximity to Europe. The following passages explore the evolution of this estate.

The development of its counterpart in Europe—absolute ownership—followed a different path. In particular, the French Revolution swept away the existing, arcane property law system in France. The system that replaced it was simplified and statutory, as set forth in the French Civil Code of 1804. This Code greatly influenced the evolution of the civil law approach to property, both in Europe and beyond.

Benjamin N. Cardozo
The Nature of the Judicial Process

54–55 (1921)

Let me speak first of those fields where there can be no progress without history. I think the law of real property supplies the readiest example. No lawgiver meditating a code of laws conceived the system of feudal tenures. History built up the system and the law that went with it. Never by a process of logical deduction from the idea of abstract ownership could we distinguish the incidents of an estate in fee simple from those of an estate for life, or those of an estate for life from those of an estate for years. Upon these points, "a page of history is worth a volume of logic."

So it is wherever we turn in the forest of the law of land. Restraints upon alienation, the suspension of absolute ownership, contingent remainders, executory devises, private trusts and trusts for charities, all these heads of the law are intelligible only in the light of history, and get from history the impetus which must shape their subsequent development. I do not mean that even in this field, the method of philosophy plays no part at all. Some of the conceptions of the land law, once fixed, are pushed to their logical conclusions with inexorable severity. The point is rather that the conceptions themselves have come to us from without and not from within, that they embody the thought, not so much of the present as of the past, that separated from the past their form and meaning are unintelligible and arbitrary, and hence that their development, in order to be truly logical, must be mindful of their origins. . . .

Sir Edward Coke
The First Part of the Institutes
of the Laws of England

1–2 (1628)

Tenant in fee simple is he which hath lands or tenements to hold to him and his heires for ever. And it is called in Latin, *feodum simplex*, for *feodum* is the same that inheritance is, and *simplex* is as much as to say, lawfull or pure. And so *feodum simplex* signifies a lawfull or pure inheritance. For if a man would purchase lands or tenements in fee simple, it behooveth him to have these words in his purchase, To have and to hold to him and to his heires: for these words (his heires) make the estate of inheritance. For if a man purchase lands by these words, To have and to hold to him for ever; or by these words, To have and to hold to him and his assignes for ever: in these two cases he hath but an estate for term of life, for that there lacke these words (his heires), which words onely make an estate of inheritance in all feoffments and grants.

Notes

1. Have historical forces had greater influence on the development of property law than on other areas of law such as contracts or civil procedure? If so, what makes property law particularly susceptible to these forces?

2. The passage from Coke demonstrates the importance of using the correct words to create estates in land. Even by the seventeenth century, there was a well-established distinction between a fee simple and a life estate. Fee simple estates are often described as perpetual or of infinite duration. They are the estates from which all other estates are carved. How can a mortal person have an estate of infinite duration?

B. BUNDLES OF RIGHTS

Under the "bundle of rights" theory in the common law system, owners are viewed as having various rights that can be asserted over land, tangible objects, and other items of property. These include the right to use and enjoy, the right to exclude, and the right to transfer. In the following passages, Hohfeld examines the bundle of rights that constitute fee simple absolute, while Aubry and Rau discuss the rights that arise from "absolute ownership" in the civil law system.

Wesley Newcomb Hohfeld
**Fundamental Legal Conceptions as
Applied to Judicial Reasoning**

96–97 (1919)

Suppose, for example, that A is fee-simple owner of Blackacre. His "legal interest" or "property" relating to the tangible object that we call *land* consists of a complex aggregate of rights (or claims), privileges, powers, and immunities. First, A has multital legal rights, or claims, that *others*, respectively, shall *not* enter on the land, that they shall not cause physical harm to the land, etc., such others being under respective correlative legal duties. Second, A has an indefinite number of legal privileges of entering the land, using the land, harming the land, etc., that is, within limits fixed by law on grounds of social and economic policy, he has privileges of doing on or to the land what he pleases; and correlative to all such legal privileges are the respective legal no-rights of other persons. Third, A has the legal power to alienate his legal interest to another, i.e., to extinguish his complex aggregate of jural relations and create a new and similar aggregate in the other person; also the legal power to create a life estate in another and concurrently to create a reversion in himself; also the legal power to create a privilege of entrance in any other person by giving "leave and license"; and so on indefinitely. Correlative to all such legal powers are the legal liabilities in other persons—this meaning that the latter are subject *nolens volens* to the changes of jural relations involved in the exercise of A's powers. Fourth, A has an indefinite number of legal immunities, using the term immunity in the very specific sense of non-liability or non-subjection to a power on the part of another person. Thus A has the immunity that no ordinary person can alienate A's legal interest or aggregate of jural relations to another person; the immunity that no ordinary power can extinguish A's own privileges of using the land; the immunity that no ordinary person can extinguish A's right that another person X shall not enter on the land or, in other words, create in X a privilege of entering on the land. Correlative to all these immunities are the respective legal disabilities of other persons in general.

Charles Aubry & Charles Rau
Droit Civil Français

Volume II, 173–176 (7th ed., 1961) (1966 translation)

The owner has the power to subject the thing belonging to him to any use compatible with its nature. He is authorized to receive all the profits, income or other benefits which the thing can produce or procure.... Finally, the owner is free to change the nature of the thing, lessen its value or destroy it. He can change the mode of land cultivation, turn arable land into pasture or vineyard, or vice versa, cultivate forest land and erect any structure above or below [the] surface, all the way to the limits of his land.... Although the exercise of these various rights of ownership is subject to the condition that it must not interfere with the ownership of another and, if the property involved has been classified as historical monument, that it will not be violated..., the mere fact that the exercise deprives a third person of some advantage or benefit does not give a cause of action for damages.... Ownership includes the power to undertake any legal transactions of which the thing is susceptible. He can lease it, alienate it gratuitously or for consideration, and if the thing is an immovable, burden it with servitudes or mortgages. He can even give up his ownership by simply abandoning the property, without transfer to another person.

The power to alienate is of public order; the owner can not in principle, renounce it by contract; a prohibition to alienate imposed by the donor on the donee, or by a testator on a legatee, has only limited effect....

The owner has the power to exclude all third persons from any use, enjoyment or disposal of his property and to take all convenient measures. He can, especially, surround his estate by walls, ditches or other enclosures, provided he respects the servitudes with which it is burdened.

Notes

1. What are the main similarities between these two views about the rights that constitute ownership? What are the main differences?

2. Does the common law view include the right to abandon property in general? To abandon real property? Why might the common law and civil law differ concerning the right to abandon real property?

C. ABSOLUTE OWNERSHIP IN CIVIL LAW SYSTEMS

Civil law systems have no legal category called "fee simple absolute." Instead, "absolute ownership" of property in these systems has expressed itself in very different ways.

Ugo Mattei
Basic Principles of Property Law:
A Comparative Legal and Economic
Introduction

13–14 (2000)

Feudalism, politically defeated by the birth of the modern state, did not leave traces on the structure and taxonomy of the civilian law of property. Perhaps because the law of property had never dealt with so many individual transactions, the French Revolution was remarkably effective in giving technical content to its antifeudal crusade. In France, Italy, or Germany, the division of proprietary interests that is the essence of the theory of estate (and trust law) raises a number of problems, since it violates several taboos of civil law thinking.

First, there is the so-called unitary theory of property rights. During the French Revolution, it became fashionable to consider the division of property rights as characteristic of feudalism. As a consequence, it was thought that the number of restricted property rights had to be strictly controlled and limited. The *numerus clausus* theory was developed, stating that dividing interests in property must be strictly confined to a small number of well-defined types. Although this idea was largely the product of the folklore and ideology of the French Revolution and lacked a well-articulated rationale, it enjoyed tremendous success, even more than the Napoleonic Code (the document which many jurists say incorporates this idea).

The Napoleonic Code, or French Civil Code of 1804, is an important source of law throughout the civil law world. Article 544 is the classic definition of property in the civil law tradition. However, Article 913 imposes a limit on the scope of property rights; it restricts the disposition of property so that a portion of a person's property must go to descendants. This doctrine is called "forced heirship" and is discussed in *Succession of Louis Lauga, Sr.*, which follows the code provisions.

The forced heirship doctrine is one of the differences between ownership in common law and civil law systems. For example, a father in New York holding fee simple absolute in land can generally transfer this estate to anyone he chooses, subject to marital property laws that may give his wife a partial share. But a father in France who has absolute ownership of a parcel of land must retain part of that property for his children.

French Civil Code of 1804

Article 544. Property is the right to enjoy and to dispose of things in the most absolute manner, provided that one does not undertake a usage prohibited by law.

Article 913. Free gifts, whether by acts during life, or by will, shall not exceed the half of the property of the disposer, if he leave at his decease but one legitimate child; the third part if he leave two; the fourth part if he leave three or more of them.

SUCCESSION OF LOUIS LAUGA, SR.
Supreme Court of Louisiana
624 So.2d 1156, 1159–1162, 1172 (1993)

DENNIS, J.

[Two children brought an action against their father's estate to annul his will, which left the entire estate to a third child. Plaintiffs challenged the constitutionality of a statute that redefined forced heirship to include only descendants who were under age 23 or incompetent. The trial court entered judgment for plaintiffs, and the Supreme Court affirmed.]

Civil law systems typically protect children of *all* ages, and sometimes ascendants and other descendants, from disinheritance by securing to them a minimum share of their decedent's estate which cannot be defeated by mortis causa or inter vivos gratuitous donations.... From its beginning in about 1700, Louisiana's forced heirship doctrine followed this basic civil law concept while modeling its particular provisions on French and Spanish sources. In 1921, forced heirship was elevated to the status of a constitutionally protected legal institution. Article IV, § 16 of the 1921 state constitution contained a prohibition declaring that "[n]o law shall be passed abolishing forced heirship...." Subsequently, our courts and commentators interpreted this provision not only as a limitation upon the power of the legislature to abolish forced heirship and as a grant of constitutional protection to the legal institution to further important social purposes but also as a guarantee of the individual constitutional right of every child to a forced portion of his or her decedent's estate....

The doctrine of forced heirship has prevailed in Louisiana since its colonization by French settlers at the beginning of the eighteenth century. Continuously during Louisiana's history as a colony, territory, and state, its laws have imposed a general restriction upon every person's ability to gratuitously dispose of property, i.e., in cases when the disposing person had an heir who was his lineal relative, his gratuitous dispositions could affect only a portion of his estate; the balance was reserved to his descendant or ascendant heirs, who were called forced heirs. . . .

In the Louisiana Civil Code of 1808, properly styled the Digest of the Civil Laws now in Force in the Territory of Orleans, the redactors reiterated the old Spanish rules regarding [forced heirship]. A parent's donations either inter vivos or mortis causa could not exceed one-fifth of his property to the prejudice of his children, and those of a child could not exceed one-third to the prejudice of the parents.

When the Code was revised in 1825, the disposable portion was increased and, in keeping with the French Civil Code, graduated in accordance with the number of children. Children of all ages were protected from disinheritance by being guaranteed a minimum share of the decedent's estate that could not be defeated by will or inter vivos gratuitous disposition. Such dispositions could not exceed two-thirds of the estate if the decedent left one child; one-half if he left two children; and one-third if he left a greater number. . . . This provision was carried over into the Revised Civil Code of 1870 as Article 1493. . . .

The history of Article IV, § 16 indicates that the proponents of the 1921 constitutional provision recognized the importance of preserving the legal institution of forced heirship, especially its core principle of equality of heirship, in order to further significant social and economic interests. . . . The proponents of this provision perceived the constitutional preservation of forced heirship and the principles it encompasses as a means of ensuring several important private and public policies: equitable distribution and equality of heirship among children; lessening of disputes, will contests and other wasteful litigation; harmony and solidarity of the family; and continued prevention of the cumulation of excessively large fortunes through primogeniture and entailment. . . . [The] convention delegate who introduced the ordinance to limit the legislative powers . . . later explained the economic and social principles which its proponents sought to further by prohibiting the abolishment of forced heirship or the legalization of substitutions, fidei commissa or unlimited trusts:

The most remarkable of the economic principles enunciated in the Civil Code, however, deals with the very current problem of the maldistribution of wealth and its unhealthy accumulation. Mindful of the evils in democracy, one of the great purposes of the Code is the prevention of this disease. The strict provisions of the Code governing the right of a testamentary disposition, in the institution of the doctrine of forced heirship and its elaborate provisions insuring equality of heirs, all flow from the same desire of obviating the possibility of the passing of great estates into single hands. The provision of the Code prohibiting fidei commissa and substitutions—that is to say, the prohibition of trust estates—was likewise designed to keep in commerce the flow of wealth incident on death.

So primogeniture, entailment, trust, and every other form through which fortunes might be held intact despite death are interdicted by the Civil Code of Louisiana. The agency of death thus performs its normal function—it releases the grasp of the possessor over worldly accumulation. It distributes, vests ownership and right of untrammeled disposition, breaks up the estate, and thus gives full play to the natural rule expressed in the homely proverb that it is but three generations from shirt-sleeves to shirt-sleeves. Thus the law does not stunt the natural instinct of acquisition nor interfere with the normal desire to accumulate for one's own posterity. It does not seek to confiscate nor to destroy. It simply says to the individual: "You have no natural right to retain the dead hand on your fortune. You must distribute and distribute in full ownership."

These three—forced heirship, equality of heirs, prevention of trusts—together form a system of protection of democracy from too powerful wealth, which, if they had [been] in effect in the nation from the period of the intensive industrial development since the Civil War, would have obviated the evils now sought to be remedied by more drastic means by national authority.

. . .

For the reasons assigned, the judgment of the trial court is amended so as to declare unconstitutional Act No. 788 of 1989, Act No. 147 of 1990, and Civil Code article 1493 as amended by those Acts. As amended, the trial court judgment is affirmed.

Notes

1.   After the decision in *Lauga*, all children of a deceased parent were considered to be forced heirs in Louisiana. In 1995, responding to this decision, the state legislature obtained the two-thirds vote necessary to amend the Louisiana Constitution and reinstate the age and

competency limitations on forced heirship. To what extent does this process illustrate: (a) different notions of property between the civil law and common law systems? and (b) different views of the link between property and political, economic, and social structures?

2. How is absolute ownership of property limited by the civil law doctrine of forced heirship, when compared to fee simple ownership without the doctrine?

3. In light of the common law approach that prevails in most of the United States, how convincing are the court's policy justifications for maintaining forced heirship?

Chapter 4

NUMERUS CLAUSUS

In both the common law and civil law worlds, an owner of property has many rights, as the materials in Chapter 3 illustrate. But there are limits. For example, an owner may not create a property interest that is not recognized by law. In the civil law system, this limit is expressed in Latin as the *numerus clausus* ("closed number") doctrine. Although the common law system seems to reflect the same doctrine, no name for it exists in common law sources. This illustration serves to remind all of us engaged in global legal work that terminology and categories may be fundamentally different between systems. Indeed, one system may have a precise label for a concept, while another system may view it as an underlying assumption, too fundamental to merit a name.

A. *NUMERUS CLAUSUS* DEFINED

Bernard Rudden
Economic Theory v. Property Law: The *Numerus Clausus* Problem

Oxford Essays in Jurisprudence, Third Series 239, 241–244 (1987)

. . . In all 'non-feudal' systems with which I am familiar (whether earlier, as at Rome, or later), the pattern is (in very general terms) similar: there are less than a dozen sort of property entitlements. Three confer possession, either now or later, good against strangers: fee (ownership, full or bare), life estate (usufruct), and lease. The non-possessory and non-security real rights will be given the name 'servitudes'. The common law fragments this class into an overlapping host of easements, profits, restrictive covenants, equitable servitudes, real covenants, land obligations. The classical Roman texts mostly give examples: way, water, light and so on. . . .

In very general terms, then, all systems limit, or at least greatly restrict, the creation of real rights: 'fancies' are for contract, not property. . . .

The codified systems

Many systems enact as a basic rule the proposition that 'no real rights can be created other than those provided for in this Code or other legislation' (Japanese CC 175; similar provisions occur in Argentine CC 2536, Ethiopian CC 1204(2), Korean CC 185, Louisiana CC 476–8 . . .). As far as I know, only one country then enacts the logical corollary. The Argentine CC 2536 continues:

> Any contract or testamentary disposition which constitutes or modifies real rights otherwise than as recognized by this Code is valid only, if at all, as a constitution of personal rights.

The primary sources of the Romans, French, and Germans are not so explicit, but a strong current of doctrine and case law insists that the only entitlements permitted to prevail against strangers are those listed in the law and patterned as described above....

The uncodified systems

Similar assertions are often to be found as the major premise of a common-law syllogism. The best known are:

Brougham LC: 'There are certain known incidents to property and its enjoyment; among others, certain burthens . . . recognized by the law . . . But it must not therefore be supposed that interests of a novel kind can be devised . . .'

Pollock CB: 'A new species of incorporeal hereditament cannot be created at the will and pleasure of an individual owner of an estate; he must be content to take the sort of estate and the right to dispose of it as he finds the law settled by decisions, or controlled by act of Parliament.'

Wilde B.: 'It is a well settled principle of law that new modes of holding and enjoying real property cannot be created.'

Bramwell B.: 'New rights of property cannot be created.'

Holmes J.: 'The question remains whether, even if we make the further assumption that the covenant was valid as a contract between the parties, it is of a kind that the law permits to be attached to land . . .'

Holmes O.W.: 'New and unusual burdens cannot be imposed on land. It strikes our ears strangely to hear a right of services from an individual called a right of property as distinguished from a contract.'

Olney J.: 'Such servitudes ... are opposed to the rule that the owner of land may not create new and heretofore unknown estates.'

. . .

Notes

1. What does Rudden mean when he writes that " 'fancies' are for contract, not property"? The example of creating a "time-sharing" interest in a watch, an example used by several scholars, illustrates this point. "[S]uppose A wants to create a 'time-share' in [a] watch, which would allow B to use the watch on Mondays but only on Mondays (with A retaining for now the rights to the watch on all other days). . . . A and B are not permitted by the law of personal property to create a *property right* in the use of the watch on Mondays only and to transfer this property right from A to B." Thomas W. Merrill & Henry E. Smith, *Optimal Standardization in the Law of Property: The* Numerus Clausus *Principle,* 110 Yale L.J. 1, 27 (2000).

2. Rudden presents the reasons commonly used to justify a limited number of property interests, including: (a) an absence of demand for new forms of property; (b) the problem of notice to purchasers; (c) the issue of "pyramiding"—that each new owner may add new layers of restrictions; (d) philosophical concerns; and (e) various economic reasons. As the title of his article suggests, the economic reasons have become particularly important to scholars. Rudden's work challenges the notion that the *numerus clausus* doctrine is economically necessary; he reports that "the current literature offers no economic explanation of the *numerus clausus*, but seems largely to ignore its existence." Rudden, *supra* at 261.

3. Since Rudden's article, several scholars have attempted to address the challenge he raises. For example, in the article cited in Note 1, Merrill and Smith provide an economic approach to *numerus clausus*; they observe that the costs of measuring and finding out about variations in property interests do produce the standardization reflected in the principle. They conclude: "The *numerus clausus* principle can be seen from this perspective as a device that moves the system of property rights in the direction of the optimal level of standardization." Merrill & Smith, *supra* at 40.

4. The *numerus clausus* doctrine may frustrate the intention of an unwary grantor. What was the property interest created in the next case? How did the doctrine operate to defeat it? Why did the court decide not to enforce this "fancy"?

B. *NUMERUS CLAUSUS* IN COMMON LAW PRACTICE

KAJO CHURCH SQUARE, INC. v. WALKER

Court of Appeals of Texas
2003 WL 1848555, at 1–5

GRIFFITH, J.

Don and Patsy Walker and Joe and Meriam Eakin (hereinafter collectively referred to as "Appellees") filed a declaratory judgment action in which they pleaded that they had a life estate or a leasehold for life in certain property owned by Kajo Church Square, Inc. and the Kajo Trust (hereinafter collectively referred to as "Kajo")....

Appellees transferred ownership of two parcels of land in Whitehouse, Texas to Grace Covenant Fellowship Church ("Grace" or "church"). Part of the transfer was a gift, and part was a sale. The deed does not include any language which would indicate that the couples had reserved a life estate for themselves. Contemporaneously, the church leased one of the parcels of land back to Appellees. The document stated that the lease would continue in effect until "the date of death of the last of the Lessees to die."

Four years later, the church sold the acreage to Kajo Church Square, Inc. and the church building to Kajo Trust. One week after purchasing the property, Kajo notified Appellees that it was terminating the lease. The two couples filed a declaratory judgment action against Kajo, asking the court to declare the rights and responsibilities of all parties as to the property. They sought a declaratory judgment that they had retained a life estate interest in the property or, in the alternative, that their lease of the property was a lease for life, terminable only upon the death of all four Appellees. They also pleaded that if, in fact, the property interest was a lease, Kajo breached that contract when it gave Appellees notice of termination of that lease. Further, Appellees asked that the original transaction between Appellees and Grace be rescinded if the court construed the lease to be a tenancy at will.

Appellees filed a motion for summary judgment, as did Kajo. Both motions averred that there were no disputed issues of material fact, and that each of the parties was entitled to judgment as a matter of law. The trial court granted Appellees' motion and denied Kajo's, which decisions Kajo now appeals....

Life Estate, Leasehold for Life, or Tenancy at Will

In its first two issues, Kajo argues that the trial court erred when it construed the nature of Appellees' interest in the property.

The cardinal rule applied in construing written instruments, including deeds, is to give effect to the intention of the parties as expressed by the language used by them in the instrument.... When the terms of a deed plainly and clearly disclose the intention of the parties, or the language used is not fairly susceptible to more than one interpretation, the intention of the parties must be ascertained by the court as a matter of law from the language used in the writing.... This rule of construction is known as the "four corners" rule.... In seeking to ascertain the intention of the parties, the court attempts to harmonize all parts of the deed.... If there is no ambiguity, extrinsic evidence may not be considered in determining the parties' intent. ... Further, in the absence of reservations, exceptions or other limitations reducing the estate conveyed, a deed conveys to the grantee the entire estate owned by the grantor at the time of the conveyance....

In its [sic] motion for summary judgment Appellees attached the deed transferring ownership of the property from Appellees to Grace. The deed states the following:

> Grantors, for the consideration and subject to the reservations from and exceptions to conveyance and warranty, grant, sell, and convey to Grantees the property, together with all and singular the rights and appurtenances thereto in any wise belonging, to have and hold it to Grantees, Grantees' heirs, executor, administrators, successors, or assigns forever.

Appellees also attached the condition statement signed by Kajo when it purchased the property from Grace. It gives notice to Kajo that the "[s]mall out-building on west side of premises and parking lot between said building and E. Main Street are subject to a life estate use agreement between The Church and previous owners."

As illustrated above, there is no language in the deed of record evidencing Appellees' alleged life estate interest in the property. Further, the deed is not ambiguous; consequently, extrinsic evidence such as the condition statement may not be used to determine the intent of the parties. We hold, therefore, that Appellees failed to conclusively establish that it [sic] was entitled to judgment as a matter of law. Because Appellees failed in their burden, it was not necessary for Kajo to show that there was a disputed material fact issue precluding summary judgment.... We hold, therefore, that the trial court erred when it granted Appellees' motion on this issue.

As did Appellees, Kajo attached the deed transferring ownership of the property from Appellees to Grace to its motion for summary judgment....

In response to Kajo's motion for summary judgment, Appellees attached the condition statement described above.... [S]ince the deed is not ambiguous, extrinsic evidence may not be used to determine the intent of the parties; therefore, Appellees failed to establish any genuine question of material fact in its [sic] response. Consequently, the trial court erred when it denied Kajo's motion for summary judgment on this issue. Accordingly, we hold that Appellees did not retain a life estate in the property and that Grace conveyed a fee simple interest in the land.

Also in its [sic] summary judgment motion, and in the alternative, Appellees maintained that the lease creates a leasehold for life. They attached the lease which they signed concurrently with the transfer of the property to Grace, which states that "... the said Lessor does by these presents Lease and Devise unto the said Lessee the following described property ... for the term of January 1, 1996 and ending at the date of death of the last of the Lessees to die...." They also attached the lease assignment between Grace and Kajo, which states: "Assignee agrees to assume Assignor's obligations under the Lease and to accept the premises in their present 'AS IS' condition." ... Additionally, Appellees offered the warranty deed from Grace to Kajo as evidence that Kajo accepted the transfer of the property from Appellees to Grace with all encumbrances, including the lease for life. With the above-described evidence, Appellees showed that there was no disputed fact issue as to a lease for life, and that they were entitled to judgment as a matter of law.

However, in its response, Kajo argued that the lease creates no more than a tenancy at will. It cited *Nitschke v. Doggett* ... for the proposition that the lease document does not, in fact, create a lease or tenancy for life. In *Nitschke,* the court stated the following: "That we shall die, we know; only the hour of death's arrival is unknown. But, an event certain to occur, but uncertain as to the time of its occurrence, as the death of appellee, may not be used to mark the termination of a lease." ... Consequently, a lease which terminates upon the death of a lessee is a tenancy at will rather than a tenancy for life. ...

Although there is a dearth of authority to support Kajo's position, it is bolstered by landlord-tenant law, which recognizes only four types of leases: the term of years, the periodic tenancy, the tenancy at will, and the tenancy at sufferance. Thomas W. Merrill and Henry E. Smith, *Optimal Standardization in the Law of Property: The* Numerus Clausus *Principle,* 110 Yale L.J. 1, 11 (2000) .... Thus, a leasehold for life is not a recognized property right. Therefore, as a matter of law, the lease constitutes a tenancy at will. Consequently, the trial court erred when it granted Appellees' motion and denied Kajo's motion on this issue. Accordingly, we hold that Kajo owns the property in fee simple, encumbered only by a tenancy at will....

Notes

1. Why didn't the court permit a leasehold for life? What unstated policies support the court's rejection of this new kind of property interest?

2. Do you think that attaching the name *"numerus clausus doctrine"* to the reason for rejecting the new property interest makes it easier for a judge to resolve this case? If so, how might this illustration be expanded to our general understanding of the use of terms and concepts in different legal systems?

3. In *Garner v. Gerrish*, 473 N.E.2d 223 (N.Y. 1984), the Court of Appeals of New York interpreted the following language that defined the term of a lease: "for and during the term of *quiet enjoyment* from the *first* day of *May*, 1977 which term will end—*Lou Gerrish has the privilege of termination [sic] this agreement at a date of his own choice.*" The court held that this language created a life tenancy terminable at the will of the tenant, Lou Gerrish, not a tenancy at will. The opinion states: "Thus, the lease will terminate, at the latest, upon the death of the named lessee." *Id.* at 225. Does this suggest that some common law courts will apply the *numerus clausus* doctrine with less vigor? Would the *Garner* court have reached the same conclusion if the language of the lease were "for and during the term of the life of Lou Gerrish"?

Chapter 5

FUTURE INTERESTS

Like the system of estates, our law of future interests is a product of the historical development of land law in England. The common law recognized a vast array of future interests, which provided great flexibility in controlling the disposition of property after the owner's death.

Consider an example. Suppose that O owns fee simple absolute in Blackacre, a farm in a common law nation. O devises Blackacre to A for life, and then to B and his heirs. Upon O's death, A has a life estate, and B has an indefeasibly vested remainder in fee simple absolute. B's remainder is fully valid, so B receives fee simple absolute when A dies. Thus, the common law would allow O's will to control the transfer of Blackacre after A's death—even though O is already dead.

In contrast, the civil law system evolved along quite a different path. Legislation in civil law nations traditionally placed clear limitations on the duration of rights that a common law lawyer would call "future interests." Now suppose that O has absolute ownership of Noirhectare, a farm in a civil law nation. O devises Noirhectare to A for life, and then to B. In the civil law system, O's attempt to control the passage of property after A's death is not permitted. From this perspective, O is attempting to "substitute" his will for the law's requirement that A's property must go to A's children and other descendents when A dies. Such substitutions are prohibited. As a result, O's entire devise may be invalid, with neither A nor B receiving any interest under the devise.

A. LIMITATIONS ON FUTURE INTERESTS

Phanor J. Eder
**A Comparative Survey of Anglo–American
and Latin–American Law**

112–117 (1950)

The strict common law also paid a great deal of attention to future interests in real property. Indeed, future interests, in contrast to Latin–American law, constitute a large part of our law of property. Latin–American textbooks and commentaries pay very little attention to this topic. The Codes contain only scattered articles, usually under the topics of conditional obligations, succession, and gifts. Future interests are not dealt with in the chapters or titles that deal with property. While various forms of entail...were known to the earlier Spanish law, they were abolished by the Constitutions and Codes, and in general restraints on alienation are prohibited. The period of our Rule against Perpetuities is more liberal than the Latin–American prohibitions against restraints on alienation.

In contrast to Latin America, long-term leases are common.... The Argentine Civil Code provides that a contract of lease cannot be entered into for a term exceeding ten years. Any lease for a longer term shall terminate at the end of ten years. The Mexican Code places a limit of ten years for residence, fifteen for commercial uses, and twenty for industrial uses....

Under the Argentine Code, donors may expressly reserve the "reversion" in case of death of the donee or of the donee and his heirs. But a conditional reversion is good only in favor of the donor himself; it is not good if it is to the heirs of the donor or to a third person. Hence the Argentine "reversion" is quite different from our remainders and reversions. The Brazilian Code permits a reversion in gifts only for the event that the donor survives the donee. The Argentine Code further provides that a testator can substitute...someone to the heir or legatee first named in the will in case such heir of legatee refuses or cannot accept the inheritance. Only this kind of substitution is permitted in wills. The dispositions of a will under which a third person is given a whole or part of what remains of the inheritance after the death of the instituted heir or by which a whole or part of the inheritance is declared inalienable are void. The Colombian Civil Code provides that gifts can be made only to a person living at the time of the gift, or, if made under a suspensive condition (analogous to a condition precedent), living at the time of the performance of the condition. The same holds true for suspensive conditions in wills, but in the case of both gifts and wills exception is made in favor of persons not born, if expected to exist and they do come into existence within thirty years.

The thirty-year period is quite usual in the Codes as the maximum time permitted to suspend alienation....

The Argentine Civil Code contains many provisions prohibiting inalienability or restricting it to very short periods in addition to the one concerning the duration of leases already cited.

By a Spanish law of 1821, in force in Mexico, entails and substitutions...were abolished, and this prohibition was continued in subsequent legislation. The present Mexican Civil Code, except as modified by the trust statute, forbids dispositions that contain prohibitions on alienation, most remainders, and charges on income in favor of more than one person successively.

Latin American law then prohibits interests which last *too long*. Our Rule against Perpetuities is much more liberal....

The Rule against Perpetuities must be distinguished from the rules against what we call restraints on alienation, though like these rules it springs from the same general public policy against withholding property from commerce. A restraint on alienation is some attempted provision that, even after an interest has become *vested*, prevents the owner thereof from disposing of it absolutely or from disposing of it in a particular way or to a particular purpose. ... An interest which is void under the Rule against Perpetuities fails because it vests too remotely. It may be and usually is alienable at all times....

Vesting, or a vested right, is analogous but not exactly equivalent to the Latin–American acquired right (derecho adquirido). In the common law, a future estate can vest in interest before it comes into actual possession of the person entitled to it; this distinction, this somewhat metaphysical conception, is incorporated in the Rule against Perpetuities. A remainder complies with the requirement of the rule as soon as it becomes vested, regardless of when the remainderman is to come into possession. Thus in a devise to A for life, remainder to A's children for their lives (including children not yet born), remainder to B (a person in existence), B's interest is good: it is presently *vested* though B may not come into possession until the death of a child of A yet unborn—a point well beyond the period of perpetuities. Even if B should die before all A's children die, it is still a vested remainder because B's heirs would take the property. On the other hand, if the grant is to A for life and if B survives A, to B in fee simple, B has a contingent interest only because it is uncertain whether he will survive A. Such a provision in a will, I believe, would be invalid everywhere in Latin America unless B comes into possession within ten, twenty, or thirty years.

Similarly, possibilities of reverter or reversion do not offend the Rule against Perpetuities. They are in theory vested. Thus: A testator devises real estate to a church to hold so long as the property is used for church purposes. If the prescribed use ceases the property reverts to T or to his heirs, even if this occurs centuries later. This also, I believe, would be impossible in any Latin–American country. A resolutory condition must take effect within a relatively short period of time, ten, twenty, or thirty years.

Notes

1.   Eder points out that, while future interests "constitute a large part" of the Anglo–American law of property, they are comparatively rare in civil law systems. Why?

2.   As the Eder passage indicates, the civil law has a more restrictive regime for permitted periods of inalienability, permitted periods for leaseholds, and the creation of interests that common law lawyers would call "future interests." What policies do these rules reflect?

3.   Should owners have the autonomy to create whatever future interests they wish? Why should the law intervene in these decisions?

B. FUTURE INTERESTS ON THE BORDER BETWEEN THE COMMON LAW AND CIVIL LAW SYSTEMS

One of the great inventions of the common law was the trust. By splitting legal title to property (held by a trustee) from equitable title (held by the trust beneficiaries), the trust provided landowners with added flexibility in the disposition of their property after death. The trust expanded the range of common law future interests by allowing the creation of "equitable" future interests.

In recent decades, some civil law nations have adopted legislation that creates devices similar to the common law trust. Yet the law in those nations has long prohibited any "substitution," as illustrated by the Noirhectare example above. What happens when the newly-created civil law trust meets the traditional prohibition on substitution? The clash between these two concepts is reflected in the next case, where the court considers whether the provisions of a new trust law will save a disposition of property that would otherwise fail under the prohibition on substitution.

CRICHTON v. GREDLER

Supreme Court of Louisiana
235 So.2d 411, 412–422 (1970)

SUMMERS, J.

Plaintiffs Gloria Crichton McGehee and Powell Crichton, Jr., are a niece and nephew, respectively, of Kate Crichton Gredler the decedent. They petitioned for the annulment of the last will and testament of the decedent, contending primarily that the will contained a substitution prohibited by the Constitution and Civil Code of Louisiana. The trial court refused to annul the will. On appeal the Second Circuit reversed. ...

The contested will is in olographic [handwritten] form and is dated March 6, 1963. After provisions revoking all prior wills, appointing Thomas Crichton, Jr., her brother, as executor and directing the payment of her debts, the will provides:

> ...[A]nd I do hereby give and bequeath to the said Thomas Crichton jr. as trustee for the benefit of his two sons, my nephews, Thomas Crichton Third, and John H. Crichton, all the rest, residue and remainder of my property, both real and personal ...; [the property] shall thereafter be held in an undivided one-half interest in each of the aforementioned two trusts, each trust created and named for its above named beneficiary, and both trusts shall be Louisiana trusts.... In the event that either beneficiary, Thomas Crichton third or John Hayes Crichton be not living when this trust is terminated, both income and corpus of such said trust shall be paid over or conveyed by Trustee to the child or children of said deceased beneficiary in equal, undivided portions. In event that neither a beneficiary nor his child or children are living upon the termination of this trust, then said income and corpus shall be paid over or conveyed by the Trustee to the other trust beneficiary or, if he be not living, then to his child or children in equal or undivided portions. ...

. . .

Does the will contain a substitution? The answer is yes. Prohibited substitutions are defined by the law. Prior to its amendment in 1962, Article 1520 of the Civil Code read:

> Substitutions and Fidei commissa are and remain prohibited. Every disposition by which the donee, the heir, or legatee is charged to preserve for or to return a thing to a third person is null, even with regard to the donee, the instituted heir or the legatee.

. . .

In construing Article 1520, our cases have formulated a distinction between the substitution and the fidei commissum and clarified the definitions applicable to each. ... [In *Succession of Reilly*, Chief Justice O'Niell] wrote:

In more than a century of jurisprudence on the subject of substitutions and fidei commissa, prohibited by Article 1520 of the Civil Code, the distinction between them and the difference in their effect has been consistently observed. The essential elements of the prohibited substitution are that the immediate donee is obliged to keep the title of the legacy inalienable during his lifetime, to be transmitted at his death to a third person designated by the original donor or testator. Such a disposition is null even with regard to the original donee or legatee. ... A substitution is an attempt on the part of the donor or testator to make a testament for his donee or legatee along with his own will, and to substitute his own will for the legal order of succession from his donee or legatee. ...

. . .

It is to check the power of a testator to thus control the descent and distribution of his property after title has vested in the first legatee upon his death, in contravention of the laws establishing the order of inheritance, as well as to present restraints upon the alienation of property, that the law, as a penalty, strikes down the entire disposition, the second paragraph of Article 1520 clearly providing that 'Every disposition by which the donee, the heir, or the legatee is charged to preserve for or return a thing to a third person is null even with regard to the donee, the instituted heir, or the legatee.' As pointed out in *Succession of Johnson*, ... 'in cases of prohibited substitutions the whole will is stricken with nullity whereas in cases of fidei commissa, it is only those dispositions which are tainted with that designation that are invalid,' the vital distinction being whether the instituted legatee has under the bequest the authority to alienate the title placed in him....

Our first problem is to examine the contested Gredler will in the light of these definitions of prohibited substitutions and determine whether such a substitution is present. Section 1821 of the Trust Code stipulates that 'A testamentary trust is created at the moment of the settlor's death....' The interest in the bequest of the universal legatees or principal beneficiaries of the trust also vests at the moment of the testatrix's or settlor's death.

As the will provides no term for the trusts, each of them will terminate upon the death of its respective beneficiary in accordance with Section 1833(1) of the Trust Code, providing that 'If the trust instrument stipulates no term, the trust shall terminate: (1) Upon the death of the last income beneficiary who is a natural person....' And at the death of the beneficiaries the principal devolves upon their heirs. La. Civil Code art. 940; La. Trust Code § 1972.

Thus, the two principal beneficiaries cannot be living at the time the trusts terminate, since their respective deaths, by operation of law, will be the terminating events. Nevertheless the testatrix named Thomas Crichton III and John H. Crichton as beneficiaries of the trusts created by her will, and she provided that at their death the trust properties should be paid over and conveyed to their respective children. Therefore, inasmuch as a substitution consists of successive principal interests, and of the making of a will for the first named legatee by the decedent, the present will provides for the successive interests to vest after the termination of the trust. The substitution is therefore not 'in trust' as the Trust Code could permit. It is, instead, out of trust. Moreover, in so providing the testatrix makes the will of the first legatees. In so doing she creates a substitution prohibited by law.

What, then, is the effect of the 1962 amendment to Section 16 of Article IV of the Constitution, the 1962 amendment to Article 1520 of the Civil Code and the Louisiana Trust Code on the substitution determined to exist in this will under prior law?

The 1962 amendment to Section 16 of Article IV of the Constitution abolished many of the restraints theretofore imposed upon trusts, but it retained the traditional prohibition against substitutions except as they might be authorized by the Legislature. Insofar as it is pertinent here, the amendment provides: 'Substitutions not in trust are and remain prohibited; but trusts may contain substitutions to the extent authorized by the Legislature.'

In like manner, the amendment to Article 1520 of the Civil Code retained the prohibition against substitutions except insofar as substitutions might be permitted in the laws relating to trust. As amended in 1962 the Article now reads:

> Substitutions are and remain prohibited, except as permitted by the laws relating to trusts. Every disposition not in trust by which the donee, the heir, or legatee is charged to preserve for and to return a thing to a third person is null, even with regard to the donee, the instituted heir or the legatee.

The amendments of 1962, therefore, do nothing to legitimate substitutions, except insofar as they authorize the Legislature to permit substitutions in trust, that is, the Trust Code of 1964 or other legislative acts must implement the authorizations contained in the amended Constitution and Civil Code.

Despite Section 1723 declaring that 'A disposition authorized by this Code may be made in trust although it would contain a prohibited substitution if it were made free of trust.', study of the Trust Code discloses no provision permitting a substitution in trust. ... To the contrary, Sections 1971 and 1972 of the Trust Code embody prohibitions which effectively prevent the creation of substitutions in trust:

§ 1971. The interest of a principal beneficiary is acquired immediately upon the creation of a trust, subject to the exceptions provided in this Code.

§ 1972. Upon a principal beneficiary's death, his interest vests in his heirs or legatees, subject to the trust, except as to class trusts. . . .

When the trust is created in the ordinary situation, therefore, the interest of a principal beneficiary must be acquired immediately upon the creation of that trust. (La. Trust Code § 1971). The provisions of the will of Mrs. Gredler violated this rule. By providing that upon termination of each trust, if the named beneficiary thereof is not living, the trust property is to be delivered to the child or children of the deceased beneficiary, and in the absence of a living child or children to successively named alternate beneficiaries, Section 1972 is also violated. At the same time the will created a prohibited substitution and as a consequence the entire will is null. . . .

SANDERS, J. (dissenting).

. . .[I]n my opinion, the present will contains no prohibited substitution. In its Report to the Legislature accompanying the Louisiana Trust Code (3A LSA XXXIX), the Louisiana State Law Institute described the features of the prohibited substitution as follows:

'(1) A double liberality, or a double disposition in full ownership, of the same thing to persons called to receive it, one after the other;

(2) Charge to preserve and transmit, imposed on the first beneficiary for the benefit of the second beneficiary;

(3) Establishment of a successive order that causes the substituted property to leave the inheritance of the burdened beneficiary and enter into the patrimony of the substituted beneficiary.'

The present trusts do not fulfill these requirements. The trustee is no beneficiary. He is a fiduciary, without full ownership of principal and income. He administers the property, not for himself but for another. Hence, there is no double disposition in full ownership, wherein the first beneficiary is required to preserve and transmit the property to a second beneficiary. . . .

In a scholarly article entitled *Substitutions, Fidei Commissa and Trusts in Louisiana Law: A Semantical Reappraisal*, 24 La. L. Rev. 439, John H. Tucker, Jr., an eminent civil law authority, has conclusively demonstrated that trusts like those in contest here are not prohibited substitutions. His conclusions are in accord with settled French doctrine and jurisprudence. . . . In nullifying the will in the present case, the majority defeats entirely the testamentary purpose of the testatrix. Such a harsh result can be avoided by applying the provisions of the Louisiana Trust Code. I would do so. For the reasons assigned, I respectfully dissent.

Notes

1. The provision of the Louisiana Constitution cited by Justice Summers links forced heirship, addressed in Chapter 3, and the prohibition of substitutions. How are these ideas related and what do they tell us about different ideas of property?

2. Why are these rules permitted to foil the intent of the testator?

3. Do you agree with the majority opinion or with the dissent? Why?

Chapter 6

MARITAL PROPERTY

A. MARITAL PROPERTY GENERALLY

The emphasis in the United States on the nuclear family helps define the nature and extent of marital property rights. While various states have taken somewhat divergent views (compare the common law system to the community property approach), the primary focus in the United States is on protecting the wife and husband. Other countries, however, may look to a broader community of interests when defining marital rights. In some societies, family membership—usually viewed as some form of extended family or tribe—has greater social and legal consequences than the marital relationship. In such societies, one might expect the treatment of marital property rights to be significantly different from ours.

QUARTEY v. MARTEY & ANOR

In the High Court, Accra, Ghana
[1959] Ghana Law Reports 377, 379–383

OLLENNU, J.

. . . [T]here is evidence led by the defendants which shows that the late H. A. Martey lived with the plaintiff for over 25 years as man and wife, and that the family of the deceased acknowledge the plaintiff as a wife of the deceased, married under the provisions of customary law. . . .

I turn now to the question of assistance which the plaintiff alleged she gave to her late husband who, she said, was out of employment and a man of straw, deserted by his first wife at the date when she got married to him. All the assistance which she said she gave her husband was an allowance of £5 a month, later increased to £10 a month; and her use of his U.A.C. Credit Custom-

47

er's Passbook to trade on his behalf. When asked how her husband who "was out of employment" could build a house valued at £6,000 on the allowance which she said she was giving him, she replied "It is only God Who can tell". She admitted, of course, that the husband was in charge of a cocoa farm at Pramkese left by his deceased father, and that he could have built the house from the proceeds of that farm. In that case the house would be family property, because by customary law any property acquired with the proceeds of family property is itself family property, and is not the self-acquired property of the member of the family so acquiring it. . . .

[B]y customary law it is a domestic responsibility of a man's wife and children to assist him in the carrying out of the duties of his station in life, e.g. farming or business. The proceeds of this joint effort of a man and his wife and/or children, and any property which the man acquires with such proceeds, are by customary law the individual property of the man. It is not the joint property of the man and the wife and/or the children. The right of the wife and the children is a right to maintenance and support from the husband and father. . . .

[I]n the absence of strong evidence to the contrary, any property a man acquires with the assistance or joint effort of his wife, is the individual property of the husband, and not joint property of the husband and the wife. There is no evidence in this case which can raise a presumption that the properties acquired by the late H. A. Martey were the joint property of himself and his wife. . . .

The customary law is, that upon a man's death intestate, his self-acquired property becomes family property, vested in his family, which will be the paternal family or the maternal family, depending upon the tribe to which the deceased belonged. Except in very rare circumstances a wife is not a member of that family. No member of the family has the inherent right to succeed the deceased; succession is a matter of appointment, or election, by the head and principal members of the family.

Nor has any member of the family an inherent right to a fixed share of the deceased's property in such a case. Therefore, even where the wife happens to be a member of her husband's family she will not be entitled to an ascertainable share of the property. The personal property is distributed among the children and other members of the family, the children getting the major share. But the real property, and certain classes of personal property, are not distributed or partitioned; they remain intact, and neither the successor nor any one member of the family can dispose of such property without the consent and concurrence of the head and principal members of the family.

By customary law the right of a widow is the right to maintenance and support by the family of her deceased husband. Her
maintenance and support remain the responsibility of the head of
the family until a certain stage of the funeral, when the family by
custom appoints a member of the family to be her new husband.
From then on, that customary husband becomes responsible for the
widow. He may not in fact live with her as man and wife, but she is
his wife de jure, and he is responsible to maintain her according to
his own standard in life, as he would maintain a wife married by
himself originally. The widow may opt not to accept the customary
husband, in which case the family's responsibility for her support
and maintenance ceases; or the family may opt to give her a send-
off, in which case, too, their responsibility would cease. In either
case, special custom must be performed to effect the determination
of the marriage of the woman into her late husband's family.

It follows that the only claim open to a widow of a marriage
according to customary law is a claim for maintenance and support.
This is based upon the principle that when the husband married
the woman into his family, he undertook responsibility for her
maintenance and support; which responsibility together with the
enjoyment of his self-acquired property (if any), falls to the lot of
his family. The widow can maintain an action for her support
against the head of the family, against the successor to her husband
(if one has been appointed according to custom), or against the
customary husband. I hold, therefore, that the plaintiff's claim to a
one-third share of the estate of her late husband is misconceived.

Notes

1. *Martey* recites the customary law of Ghana—it is the duty of
the wife and children to assist the husband in his enterprises. The
proceeds of any joint effort between the husband and wife belong solely
to the husband as his individual property, without any interest in the
wife. What is the rationale behind this approach? Does an emphasis on
the extended family validate such policies?

2. In Ghana, the importance of the extended family far exceeds
that of the nuclear family. Many communities in Ghana are matrilineal, as was the case in *Martey*. Under customary law, inheritance
rights and succession to property flow to the husband's family, rather
than to the surviving widow—even if she helped him acquire the
assets. Additionally, because children in matrilineal communities belong to their mother's lineage, they have no legal rights to inherit from
their father's estate. A man's traditional heirs are his mother, siblings,
and sister's children; a woman's children inherit from her brothers.
For a detailed discussion on the customary law of marital property
rights, see Gwendolyn Mikell, *Culture, Law, and Social Policy: Chang-*

ing the Economic Status of Ghanaian Women, 17 Yale J. Int'l L. 225 (1992).

3. In the face of increasing domestic and international pressure, Ghana has enacted a number of legal reforms regarding the property rights of women. Article 22(1) of the 1992 Ghanaian Constitution provides: "A spouse shall not be deprived of a reasonable provision out of the estate of a spouse." Further, Article 22(3)(a) states that: "Spouses shall have equal access to property jointly acquired during marriage." The Intestate Succession Law of 1985 radically changed the customary law of intestate succession and guaranteed each widow a 3/16 share of the deceased husband's property.

4. Nonetheless, women continue to face significant obstacles. The resilience of customary norms and social policies places barriers to the accomplishment of many of the intended goals. The contradiction between Western approaches and traditional norms of behavior has eviscerated the effectiveness of the new laws. For a detailed discussion of the impact of Ghana's legal reforms, see Jeanmarie Fenrich & Tracy E. Higgins, *Promise Unfulfilled: Law, Culture, and Women's Inheritance Rights in Ghana*, 25 Fordham Int'l L.J. 259 (2001).

5. International human rights law has a long-standing commitment to equal rights for women. The United Nations Charter, the Universal Declaration of Human Rights, the International Covenant on Economic, Social, and Cultural Rights, and the International Covenant on Civil and Political Rights all call for equal rights between men and women. Does international law require the equal treatment of men and women during the marriage regarding ownership and disposition of property, including property acquired during the marriage or passing under intestacy? Should it? What problems arise when international organizations try to impose their values on developing nations?

B. MARITAL PROPERTY AND SAME–SEX COUPLES

Married individuals are commonly granted rights in property owned by their spouses. Throughout most of human history, the institution of marriage has been reserved exclusively for heterosexual unions. Same-sex couples could not marry. Many societies have justified this limitation by pointing to the symbolic and spiritual significance of the marital relation and emphasizing the link between procreation, child protection, and child rearing. Since marital property rights accrue only upon becoming a "spouse," same-sex partners were excluded from a wealth of benefits provided to married couples. They had no access to such property rights as forced share, dower, tenancy by the entirety, community property, and alimony.

Within the last few decades, discussion has intensified as to whether same-sex partners should be legally recognized and whether equality between heterosexual and homosexual couples is appropriate. A few states in the United States and several countries in Europe have granted same-sex partners some of the rights of married couples. Increasingly, national legislation, transnational agreements, and international law have focused on the recognition of equal legal rights for same-sex couples.

CONVENTION FOR THE PROTECTION OF HUMAN RIGHTS AND FUNDAMENTAL FREEDOMS

(1953)

The governments signatory hereto, being members of the Council of Europe,

Considering the Universal Declaration of Human Rights proclaimed by the General Assembly of the United Nations on 10th December 1948;

Considering that this Declaration aims at securing the universal and effective recognition and observance of the Rights therein declared;

Considering that the aim of the Council of Europe is the achievement of greater unity between its members and that one of the methods by which that aim is to be pursued is the maintenance and further realisation of human rights and fundamental freedoms;

Reaffirming their profound belief in those fundamental freedoms which are the foundation of justice and peace in the world and are best maintained on the one hand by an effective political democracy and on the other by a common understanding and observance of the human rights upon which they depend;

Being resolved, as the governments of European countries which are like-minded and have a common heritage of political traditions, ideals, freedom and the rule of law, to take the first steps for the collective enforcement of certain of the rights stated in the Universal Declaration,

Have agreed as follows: . . .

Article 8—Right to respect for private and family life

1. Everyone has the right to respect for his private and family life, his home and his correspondence.

2. There shall be no interference by a public authority with the exercise of this right except such as is in accordance with the law and is necessary in a democratic society in the interests of national security, public safety or the economic well-being of the country, for the prevention of disorder or crime, for the protection of health or

morals, or for the protection of the rights and freedoms of others. . . .

Article 12—Right to marry

Men and women of marriageable age have the right to marry and to found a family, according to the national laws governing the exercise of this right. . . .

Article 14—Prohibition of discrimination

The enjoyment of the rights and freedoms set forth in this Convention shall be secured without discrimination on any ground such as sex, race, colour, language, religion, political or other opinion, national or social origin, association with a national minority, property, birth or other status. . . .

Notes

1.   The Convention for the Protection of Human Rights and Fundamental Freedoms is commonly referred to as the "European Convention on Human Rights." The Convention was opened for signatures in 1950 and entered into force in 1953. It establishes a broad network of civil and political rights and freedoms. Currently, over 40 nations are signatories. The Convention has been amended several times; these amendments affect not only its judicial procedures but also the substantive content of the rights and freedoms protected. Under Protocol 11, the European Court of Human Rights has become the primary enforcement mechanism. The decisions of the Court are legally binding on member states and the Court has the power to award damages. Any individual whose rights have been violated under the Convention by a state party can take his or her case directly to the Court. For more information on the history and current status of the Convention, see generally Jean–Francois Renucci, *Introduction to the European Convention on Human Rights* (2005).

2.   Does the right to respect for one's private and family life in Article 8 require the availability of equal property rights for same-sex couples?

3.   Why is the right to marry in Article 12 the only right made expressly dependent on the national laws of the member states?

4.   How can the prohibition on discrimination in Article 14 not be applied to discrimination against same-sex couples?

———

The following two articles provide additional context for understanding the scope of these provisions of the Convention.

Bea Verschraegen
The Right to Private Life and Family Life, the Right to Marry and to Found a Family, and the Prohibition of Discrimination

Legal Recognition of Same–Sex Couples in Europe 1–5 (2003)

Whether the European Convention on Human Rights (ECHR) is directly applicable in a Member State or not depends on the national provisions. The judgments of the European Court of Human Rights constitute precedents for future cases. Some states refer very often to the case law of the European Court of Human Rights (the Court) and anticipate further developments—(that is the case in The Netherlands), whilst other Member States take into account the case law and critically check whether their legal order complies with its provisions. . . .

Art. 8: The Right to Private Life and to Family Life

Art. 8 ECHR establishes a fundamental right to respect for private and family life. . . .

The Convention itself contains no definition of private life. The case law indicates that private life includes the possibility of developing relations with other human beings. Intimate life as well as sexual life are recognised as aspects of private life. Voluntary sexual intercourse, including homosexual intercourse, is part of private life unless such sexual activity occurs in a public sphere. A State stipulating rules in this area is interfering with private life and that interference must be justified under Art. 8 para. 2 ECHR. However, the definition of "private life" may well vary from case to case. Indeed, the Commission admitted that it is difficult to give a general definition of "respect for private life." The right to protection of personality has an important role to play as becomes clear in the cases dealing with transsexuals. Private life is interfered with when a transsexual cannot alter his/her name and identity documents after a surgery changing his/her sex. . . .

Art. 12: The Right to Marry and to Found a Family

The Court has interpreted the right to marry as referring "to the traditional marriage between persons of opposite biological sex" and the Court has also said that Art. 12 ECHR "is mainly concerned to protect marriage as the basis of the family." Consequently, Art. 12 ECHR does not protect same-sex relationships. The right to marry and to found a family under Art. 12 ECHR has been interpreted as one entity. However, in the recent transsexual cases, the Court said that the "second aspect is not . . . a condition of the first and the inability of any couple to conceive or parent a child cannot be regarded as per se removing the right to enjoy the first limb of this provision." . . .

The primary concept of the family is that of marriage. "The full protection of this family unit requires that the couple be lawfully married." Art. 12 ECHR does not impose a positive obligation upon the Member States, because it guarantees a right which can be exercised "according to the national laws governing the exercise of this right;" basically, Member States have a wide margin of appreciation in deciding "whether, or subject to what conditions, the exercise of the right ... should be permitted." Art. 12 ECHR is different from Art. 8 ECHR in that it has no "interference" clause. However, it is generally recognised that the degree of interference must be weighed against the objective sought to be achieved. The freedom of marriage may not be deprived of its "essential content." There must be a national legal basis allowing for the interference. This "legal reservation" can touch upon conditions of substantive law (discernment, capacity to marry, free consent, marriage impediments such as prohibited degrees of kinship, bigamy, public order) as well as procedural requirements (announcement of the marriage). It is up to the national law to set out the impediments to marriage. Such rules must be based on generally accepted reasons of public interest. Affinity and bigamy have been found to be justified impediments to marriage....

Art. 14: Prohibition of Discrimination

Art. 14 ECHR is not a general principle of equality. The provision prohibits discrimination when exercising one's rights pursuant to the ECHR or its Protocols. According to leading case law, Art. 14 ECHR is a part of every provision of the ECHR. Thus, it has no independent character and cannot be invoked in an isolated way. In general, the provision has a defensive character: positive duties cannot be deduced from Art. 14 ECHR. The grounds for discrimination are not enumerated in an exhaustive way, but the discrimination must be related to the person concerned. As with Art. 8 and Art. 12 ECHR, States have, of course, a margin of appreciation.

The Court examines whether the applicant was discriminated against in the specific case. There also has to be a certain degree of discrimination. As the ECHR is a "living instrument," it must be interpreted in the light of present-day conditions. If the opinions among the Member States have changed considerably, "very weighty reasons would ... have to be advanced before a difference of treatment ... could be regarded as compatible with the Convention." The Court may also consider the actual social and legal environment of the country at issue. The factual circumstances that are compared must be relevant. If they are essentially different, there is no discrimination....

To summarise: Discrimination will basically be found when a measure or provision treats a person differently from other persons in similar situations (e.g. married/unmarried mothers, legitimate/illegitimate children) and there is no objective and reasonable justification for the different treatment in the light of international treaties or other national laws. In other words, if the measure or provision does not pursue a "legitimate" interest or if there is not a "reasonable relationship of proportionality between the means employed and the aim sought to be realised." The Member States have a certain margin of appreciation in assessing whether and to what extent differences in otherwise similar situations justify different treatment.

Hans Ytterberg
All Human Beings Are Equal, But Some Are More Equal Than Others—Equality in Dignity Without Equality in Rights?

Legal Recognition of Same–Sex Couples in Europe
194–196, 204–205, 207–208 (2003)

The European Court of Human Rights in Strasbourg, in a series of judgments since 1981, has held that the European Convention for the Protection of Human Rights and Fundamental Freedoms also includes the right not to be discriminated against because of your sexual orientation. In its ground-breaking ruling in the *Dudgeon* case in 1981, the Court established a strict justification test under Article 8 of the European Convention for a difference in treatment based on sexual orientation not to be considered a violation of the Convention's prohibition on discrimination. This position of the Court has been upheld in later judgments as regards the criminal law and employment law areas as well as the family law area. . . . And for the first time the Court has declared admissible a case regarding the tenancy rights of a surviving same-sex partner.

Article 12 of the European Convention covers the right to marry. Its application to same-sex couples has not yet been tested, but in the past the Court has repeatedly held that a refusal to permit post-operative transsexuals to contract different-sex marriages in their reassigned sex is not a violation of the Convention. In a unanimous Grand Chamber ruling of 11 July 2002, however, the Court departed from its previous position in the finding that such refusals violate the right to marry under Article 12. The Court now no longer makes a reference to its earlier definition of marriage as a traditional marriage between persons of opposite biological sex. Among other things, the Court also took note of the fact that Article 9 of the recently adopted Charter of Fundamental

Rights of the European Union departs, no doubt deliberately, from the wording of Article 12 of the Convention in removing the reference to men and women. This ruling could prove to be crucial for future interpretation of Article 12 of the European Convention as also guaranteeing the right of men and women to legally marry someone of their own sex.

Nevertheless, the last few years have also seen tendencies in the opposite direction in the case law of the European Court of Human Rights in Strasbourg. In a Hungarian case where the Constitutional Court of Hungary declared constitutional the ban on gay rights organizations which allow membership also for persons below the age of 18, the Strasbourg Court declared the complaint manifestly ill founded and therefore inadmissible. The Court simply stated that such a ban pursued a legitimate aim. The Court, however, refused to consider the strict justification test established in its own case law, for such an interference with the right to private life not to be considered a violation of the Convention, if it is based on sexual orientation. . . .

Another important development during the past few years has been the adoption of the Charter of Fundamental Rights of the European Union, at the Nice summit in December of 2000. Article 21 of the Charter stipulates that any discrimination based on, for example, sexual orientation shall be prohibited. Although the European Council, after much discussion, decided to limit the direct legal value of the Charter by characterizing it as a political declaration instead of making it into a legally binding act, its importance should not be underestimated. Some of the most important legal rights of individual citizens of the Union under Community law have been created over the years, not by the adoption of legally binding texts by the Council, but through the Court of Justice's interpretation of the already existing texts of, for example, the Treaties or secondary Community legislation. . . . The day-to-day reality of many people, however, is often very different.

> In 1967, Alice B. Toklas died in Paris in extreme poverty. However, several decades earlier she and her lifelong companion, the American writer Gertrude Stein, had been described as the "most famous lesbian couple in the world." Together they organised one of the most glittering literary salons of the day, held in the couple's apartment in rue de Fleurus in Paris. In spite of the fact that they had openly shared 34 years together, Gertrude was never able to gather enough courage to use her otherwise able pen to describe their relationship in her last will. Convention, tradition and the necessary confrontation with her family, to which Gertrude had always been resigned, got in her way. After the funeral, the family descended on the pictures Gertrude had collected: fabulous Picassos, priceless

Matisses, dozens of the most avant-garde canvases. They did not even spare the couple's common property that might have provided Alice with a comfortable retirement. Instead, Alice had to serve in other people's homes until her own death, 21 years after that of Gertrude.

The story of Gertrude and Alice sheds a special light on the fact that equality in dignity is not automatically accompanied by equality in rights. The obvious fact that Gertrude and Alice had lived together as a family for almost 35 years did not give Alice any rights whatsoever when her lifelong companion passed away. It was different for the women of the numerous heterosexual couples that had gotten used to gathering in their joint home at rue de Fleurus for decades. . . .

Notes

1.   Should the European Convention impose positive obligations on member states to restrict all forms of discrimination based on sexual orientation? Why should the European Court of Human Rights consider the social and legal environment of the individual country as a factor in reaching its judgment?

2.   Ytterberg stresses the potential disconnect between the goals and language of the Convention and the case law and statutes of the individual member states. Great deference is often given by the Court when determining whether an act is in violation of the Convention, especially if based on sexual orientation. What justifies this position of the Court? Would the Court rule today that Alice B. Toklas could inherit the intestate estate of Gertrude Stein? Should its judgment depend upon whether Stein was domiciled in France, Austria, or England?

3.   Under the Austrian Rent Act, a spouse, life companion, issue, or sibling is entitled to succeed to the tenancy if the tenant dies. Siegmund Karner shared a flat with his homosexual partner. In 1994, his partner died of AIDS and the landlord brought proceedings to terminate the tenancy. The Austrian Supreme Court found that a "life companion" under the statute did not include persons of the same sex. Relying upon Article 14 of the Convention (taken together with Article 8), the European Court of Human Rights ruled that the failure to recognize Karner's right to succeed to the tenancy of his partner amounted to discrimination based upon sexual orientation. The Court noted that the Austrian Government had not offered either convincing or weighty reasons to justify its narrow interpretation of the Rent Act. *Karner v. Austria*, 38 Eur. H.R. Rep. 24 (2003).

4.   In *Frette v. France*, 38 Eur. H.R. Rep. 21 (2002), the European Court of Human Rights ruled that there had been no violation of Article 14 of the Convention when a French national's application to adopt a child was rejected under French law solely because of his

sexual orientation. The Court noted that this was a delicate issue which touched on an area where there is little common ground among member states. Because of the wide differences of national and international opinion, the Court allowed French law to determine the best interests of the child in this instance. Can this case be distinguished from *Karner*?

5. What if child psychiatrists and psychologists testify that scientific evidence shows that no negative consequences occur when a child is adopted by one or more homosexual parents? Should such evidence overcome the customs and "reasonable" laws of any member state?

6. While several European countries have granted a number of property rights to same-sex partners, others have resisted this trend. *See* Dijana Jakovac–Lozic, *Croatia's New Family Act and Its Implications on Marriage and Other Forms of Family Life*, 31 Cal. W. Int'l L.J. 83 (2000); Philip Britton, *The Rainbow Flag, European and English Law: New Developments on Sexuality and Equality*, 8 Ind. Int'l & Comp. L. Rev. 261 (1998).

Chapter 7

THE LANDLORD–TENANT
RELATIONSHIP

A. COMMON LAW TENANCIES AND THE USUFRUCT

In the United States, the leasehold is an established estate. As such, it is a vested property interest that carries with it a core bundle of rights, including the right to possess and the right to exclude. At its essence, the lease is a conveyance; and this fact colors the group of property rights that surround the transaction.

Other countries may have different approaches to the leasehold relationship. Traditionally, in Africa, ownership of land was limited to the community, commonly referred to as the "stool." Title was vested solely in the community, which apportioned the use of land to individual members. Members of the community gained only a usufruct—the right to occupy, use and enjoy the land. Compared to the tenant holding a common law leasehold in England, a community member's rights under the usufruct were more limited. While members who cultivated or built on the land were entitled to the fruits of their labor, the land's "natural fruits," such as firewood and game, could be taken by any community member. Similarly, the rights to minerals and large trees belonged to the community.

AMODU TIJANI v. SECRETARY, SOUTHERN NIGERIA
Court of Appeal of Nigeria
2 A.C. 399, 404–05 (1921)

HALDANE, J.

...[I]n interpreting the native title to land, not only in Southern Nigeria, but other parts of the British Empire, much caution is essential. There is a tendency, operating at times unconsciously, to render that title conceptually in terms which are appropriate only to systems which have grown up under English law. But this tendency has to be held in check closely. As a rule, in the various systems of native jurisprudence throughout the Empire, there is no such full division between property and possession as English lawyers are familiar with. A very usual form of native title is that of a usufructuary right, which is a mere qualification of or burden on the radical or final title of the Sovereign where that exists. In such cases the title of the Sovereign is a pure legal estate, to which beneficial rights may or may not be attached. But this estate is qualified by a right of beneficial use which may not assume definite forms analogous to estates... [T]he Indian title in Canada affords by no means the only illustration of the necessity for getting rid of the assumption that the ownership of land naturally breaks itself up into estates, conceived as creatures of inherent legal principle. Even where an estate in fee is definitely recognised as the most comprehensive estate in land which the law recognises, it does not follow that outside England it admits of being broken up. In Scotland a life estate imports no freehold title, but is simply, in contemplation of Scottish law, a burden on a right of full property that cannot be split up. In India much the same principle applies. The division of the fee into successive and independent incorporeal rights of property conceived as existing separately from the possession, is unknown. In India, as in Southern Nigeria, there is yet another feature of the fundamental nature of the title to land which must be borne in mind. The title, such as it is may not be that of the individual, as in this country it nearly always is in some form, but may be that of a community. Such a community may have the possessory title to the common enjoyment of a usufruct, with customs under which its individual members are admitted to enjoyment, and even to a right of transmitting the individual enjoyment as members by assignment *inter vivos* or by succession.

In the instance of Lagos the character of the tenure of the land among the native communities is described by Chief Justice Rayner in the Report on Land Tenure in West Africa....

> The next fact which it is important to bear in mind in order to understand the native land law is that the notion of individual ownership is quite foreign to native ideas. Land belongs to the community, the village or the family, never to the individual. All the members of the community, village, or family have an equal right to the land, but in every case the Chief or Headman of the community or village, or head of the family, has charge of the land, and in loose mode of speech is sometimes called the owner. He is to some extent in the position of a trustee, and as such holds the land for the use of the community or family. He has control of it, and any member who wants a piece of it to

cultivate or build a house upon, goes to him for it. But the land so given still remains the property of the community or family. He cannot make any important disposition of the land without consulting the elders of the community or family, and their consent must in all cases be given before a grant can be made to a stranger. . . .

Notes

1.   In what ways is the usufruct different from the common law leasehold? Is the usufruct limited to communal property systems? In Africa, the usufruct is mainly used in conjunction with communal property. The community has control of the usufruct, with customs that determine the scope of use by its members, including the right of assignment inter vivos or by succession. The individual in turn is required to perform certain customary services for the community. For an excellent examination of the customary laws applying to the usufruct, see Gordon Woodman, *The Scheme of Subordinate Tenures of Land in Ghana*, 15 Am. J. Comp. L. 457 (1967).

2.   In ancient times in Ghana, the fetish priest (called the "Tindana") was the head of state. He was in charge of the land as trustee for the people, in whom absolute ownership was vested. The Tindana's spiritual duties were inexorably connected with his control of the land. He performed sacrifices for the fertility of the land, the people, and all things on the land. The land was a highly spiritual source of life. Given this historical background, does the concept of usufruct more closely fit these customary, emotional attachments to the land than the common law tenancy? *See generally* Nii Ollennu & Gordon Woodman, Principles of Customary Land Law in Ghana (1985).

3.   What might Professor Yelpaala have meant when he wrote, "Unlike the Blackstonian power theory of property, with its focus on absolute and despotic dominion over a thing buttressed by the right of exclusion, the regime of usufructuary rights is concerned less with the power of exclusion and more with the right of access and use." Kojo Yelpaala, *Owning the Secret of Life: Biotechnology and Property Rights Revisited*, 32 McGeorge L. Rev. 111, 214 (2000).

4.   How is the usufruct—with its emphasis on use and enjoyment of the land—similar to the Native Americans' "right of occupancy," as acknowledged by Justice Marshall in *Johnson v. M'Intosh*, 21 U.S. (8 Wheat.) 543 (1823)?

B.   COMPARATIVE PERSPECTIVES ON LEASEHOLDS

1.   *Germany*

The Federal Constitutional Court of Germany has held that a tenant's interest in a rented apartment is a constitutionally-protected property right. In its decision (89 BVerfGE 1 [1993]), the Court noted:

> Housing represents for everyone the center of the private existence. The individual depends on the usage of it for the satisfaction of elementary needs of life as well as for the securing of freedom and the development of his personality. The majority of the population, however, cannot refer to property for the satisfaction [of housing needs] but is forced to rent housing. The right to occupy of the tenant in such circumstances serves functions [that are] typically being served by owned property (*Sacheigentum*). This importance of housing has been taken into account by the legislator in arranging [landlord/tenant law]. The guarantee of property unfolds its function to secure freedom in both directions. The tenant who is in compliance with his lease is being protected against losing his housing if [such a deprivation of housing] is not due to permissible justifications of the landlord. Housing, as the physical center of the free development of the personality and a free sphere of self-responsible activity, cannot be taken away by a cancellation of a lease without strong justifications.

Notes

1. Should the Constitution of the United States be amended to include housing as a fundamental right? What would the implications of such a constitutionally-protected right be? For an interesting and thoughtful treatment of this issue, see Curtis Berger, *Beyond Homelessness: An Entitlement to Housing*, 45 U. Miami L. Rev. 315 (1991).

2. The International Covenant on Economic, Social and Cultural Rights recognizes the right of all individuals to an adequate standard of living, including adequate food, clothing, and housing (Article 11). General Comment 4 stresses that "housing" includes adequate privacy, space, security, lighting, and basic infrastructure—all at a reasonable cost. Ratifying parties are required to report their housing policies and their success in meeting housing needs every four years. Should affordable housing be a basic right that every society assures its citizens?

2. *Cuba*

The housing market in Cuba is tightly controlled. Under the Urban Reform Act of 1960, leaseholds were converted from private to State ownership and the occupants were given usufructuary interests by the State. Existing rental agreements were declared illegal and the government worked to redefine the leasehold arrangement. Under Article 50 of Cuba's 1988 Housing Law, a scale for rent pricing was established. Normally, rent is capped at twenty percent of an individual's income. However, for lower income residents, rent cannot exceed ten percent of household income; and, in the "cuarterias" (slums), individuals live rent free. Rent is fixed by the municipal government and is paid monthly to the People's Savings Bank.

Notes

1.   Rent control has been hotly debated in the United States. The moral claim of allowing tenants to stay where they have lived is often contrasted with claims of inefficiency and arbitrary enactment. How is the Cuban system of rent pricing different? Could such a system work in a capitalistic economy? Do our federal housing programs attain a similar result?

2.   For an excellent discussion of Cuban property law, see Steven E. Hendrix, *Tensions in Cuban Property Law*, 20 Hastings Int'l & Comp. L. Rev. 1 (1996).

―――――

3.   *France*

In France, a residential tenancy must have a fixed term of at least three years (*Loi* No. 89–462, 1989). Rent is usually fixed for the entire term, although it can be increased annually up to the increase in the National Index of Construction Costs, calculated by the government statistical agency. While the statute contains provisions for early termination by the landlord or tenant (a tenant can provide three months' notice to quit at any time, or one month notice if she needs to vacate because of a job loss or other specified reasons), the leasehold term provides substantial stability.

Notes

1.   In her article *Renting Homes: Status and Security in the UK and France—A Comparison in the Light of the Law Commission's Proposals*, 67 Conv., Jan/Feb (2003), Jane Ball argues that France's extended fixed-term leasehold gives tenants added stability and time to plan for work and family. It also provides a more secure platform upon which to insist on tenant rights, such as property repair and habitability concerns.

2.   Should the United States be encouraged to adopt a similar provision, mandating minimum three-year residential leaseholds? Compared to this model, what are the advantages and disadvantages of

month-to-month periodic tenancies, the most common residential tenancy in the United States?

––––––––

C. LEASEHOLD REFORM

Is affordable, quality housing for all members of society possible? In 1949, Congress embraced a national goal of providing "a decent home and a suitable living environment for every American family." Housing Act of 1949, ch. 338, § 2, 63 Stat. 413 (1949); current version at 42 U.S.C. § 1441 (1994). Unfortunately, in the years that followed, there has been a lack of commitment to this goal and no developed national policy. The lack of affordable housing has been exacerbated by rising housing costs and declining household income. While the United States remains embedded in a national housing crisis, Sweden's comprehensive housing program provides a comparative model worth examining.

Deborah Kenn
**One Nation's Dream, Another's Reality:
Housing Justice in Sweden**

22 Brooklyn J. Int'l L. 63, 70, 80–82, 90–91, 93–96 (1996)

Sweden bears the banner as the international leader of affordable housing policy success. . . . The Swedish Constitution guarantees decent housing to all citizens. . . .

The initial goal of Swedish housing policy was alleviation of the extreme housing shortage. The large-scale production of housing which was needed could only be accomplished by removing housing distribution from the profit-making vagaries of the capitalist market. Creating a socialist housing market involved curtailing speculation on the cost of land and on the cost of housing on the land. In 1947, legislation gave municipalities the right to expropriate land and to control land sales by a first right of refusal. Municipal land banking provided a generous source of affordable land upon which to build nonmarket housing. Also in 1947, the Building Act legislated municipal control over the location and density of development.

Fueled by national government subsidies and municipal planning, housing development charged ahead. The capitalist system of housing production continued with private enterprise constructing housing. Social democratic principles governed distribution with nonmarket principles dominating the sale and leasing of housing. With cost controls and nonprofit markets in place, the national government committed significant financial resources to housing production, mostly in the form of below-market, fixed-rate loans. More than 90% of all housing built in Sweden since World War II has been funded by state loan subsidies.

The combination of government loans and municipal control of land and development proved a successful formula for curtailing the housing shortage. By the 1960s, Sweden boasted the highest rate of housing development in the world. In 1965, Sweden launched its "Million Dwellings Programme," ambitiously planning to build one million dwellings within ten years. The goal was truly remarkable considering the population of Sweden at the time was 7.5 million people. However, it was not considered enough merely to create dwellings. Those dwellings had to constitute decent, quality housing. Equally as important, they had to be affordable.

While the similar intent expressed in the United States Housing Act of 1949 still remains but a dream, Sweden happily achieved its stated target. By 1975, Sweden gloried in one of the highest ratios of dwellings to inhabitants in the world, at a comfortable 430 dwellings for every 1,000 people. Within its specified ten-year time frame, Sweden reached its aspirations of ending the housing shortage, improving housing conditions, and bringing housing into the realm of affordability. Gone were the days of overcrowded, unhealthy conditions for Sweden's residents. Housing standards now included realistic occupancy limits, adequate sanitation and plumbing, central heating, and modern utilities. Sweden's housing supply, in addition to being in good condition, became affordable to people. A national system of housing allowances guaranteed that a person's contribution to rent would be no more than 25% of their income. . . .

The governmental division of labor for affordable housing in Sweden proves extremely efficient. The national government legislates and administers housing policy while regional and local governments implement it. In addition to formulating housing policy, the national government provides the funds for affordable housing production and distribution. At the national level, the Ministry of Housing and Physical Planning administers and coordinates the allocation of funds among regions. There are 24 designated counties with regional governmental entities called County Administrative Boards. The County Boards act as intermediaries between the National Housing Board and municipal governments, overseeing the municipal housing plans. This dominance of regional control proves vastly superior in efficiency, fairness, and effective resource allocation than the city/suburb competition in the United States. . . .

The national and municipal governments of Sweden fund affordable housing through three different systems. Sweden has an extensive system of land banking which preserves undeveloped, affordable land for development purposes. The initial outlay of government dollars is spent on land purchases. Next, the government funds affordable housing by providing construction loans. Finally, the national and local governments bankroll housing subsidy programs to make the cost of housing affordable to all individuals and families. . . .

Over the years, legislation was enacted to strengthen municipalities' capabilities to buy, sell, and lease land. The Housing Provision and Building Acts of 1947 legitimized land banking by entrusting municipalities with the right of expropriation and the right of first refusal on land for sale. . . . In 1973, municipalities were given the right to expropriate substandard rental housing. If a municipality desires a parcel of land, a private owner must sell it at the market value ten years prior to the time of sale. . . .

Thus, in Sweden, affordable housing begins with governmentally-controlled land costs. Most developable land is removed from the speculative market by the land banking system. Having acquired land at extremely reasonable cost, the municipality can sell it for current value plus the value of any improvements. Or, as is usually the case, it can enter long term leases for the land with developers. By owning vast amounts of developable land, municipalities can control development. Enhancement of this power draws from the municipalities' ownership of nonprofit housing companies and from the legislative requirement that municipal governments create and administer master development plans. State subsidies for development are contingent upon housing developers complying with master plans which give the municipal governments considerable enforcement power. . . .

Housing tenure in Sweden is a choice between three basic forms. People looking for housing can choose to be renters, cooperative dwellers, or homeowners. The rental sector comprises 43% of the housing market, divided about equally between private and public housing. Homeowners account for 42% of housing consumers and cooperative owners represent 15% of all housing dwellers. . . .

Although rental housing occurs in both the private and public housing spheres, private rental housing operates under the control of public housing. In terms of setting rents, meeting housing standards, and determining security of tenure, the public sphere leads the way. This domination by the public housing market results from the existence of Municipal Housing Corporations (MHCs) which have acted as vehicles of the state, managing public housing since 1935. . . .

Since private rents are pegged to public rents, the ability of the public sphere to supply quality housing on a nonprofit basis results in affordable rents for both the public and private housing markets.

Private landlords have to buy into the state's system of rent-setting because their ability to seek state-subsidized housing loans depends on their adherence to that system. . . .

Rents are determined on an annual basis pursuant to negotiations between the municipal housing corporations and tenants' associations. A complicated system of rent-averaging and cost-pooling forms the basis of rent-setting. To arrive at the cost of maintaining one of its rental dwellings, the MHC determines the cost of funding and maintaining its entire stock of housing, and the cost of constructing any new housing, and then divides this figure by the number of public housing rental units. This average cost is adjusted based on individual characteristics of the dwelling, in negotiation with tenants' unions. In addition, the tenants' unions participate in this process by having access to and reviewing the records of the MHC. If any unresolvable dispute occurs in the negotiations, the National Committee on the Rental Market hears and decides appeals. Since rents are negotiated yearly to reflect the actual cost of maintaining housing and, at times, expanding the supply of housing, the nonprofitability of the housing endures.

Once rents are resolved with the MHCs, the tenants' unions must negotiate with private landlords. The "use value" determination for apartment dwellings is applied to the private housing market to achieve comparable rents. Private rental dwellings are compared to public housing dwellings in terms of their size and amenities and are priced accordingly. Comparable dwellings should have comparable rents, and all rents should be reasonable due to the nonprofit nature of the entire system. The most controversial aspect of the rent-setting system addresses the reality that older apartments and much newer apartments are priced the same. The use value system does not adjust for dwelling age. Since most public housing is relatively recent and most private housing stock is older, private housing tenants subsidize public housing tenants in their rental payments. . . .

In contrast to the United States, where private landlords can evict tenants for any but discriminatory reasons, Swedish landlords cannot evict tenants except for good reason, such as nonpayment of rent, serious tenant misconduct, or a legitimate need by the landlord for personal use of the apartment. In addition, tenants in public housing have gained considerable power over housing management decisions.

The MHCs must also provide equal opportunity housing under national policy. In Sweden, this goal means that public housing becomes available to middle income families as well as to families with limited financial means. Consequently, class barriers are broken down, with many middle income tenants residing in public housing. Single-parent households comprise a majority proportion of the overall population of public housing tenants. . . .

Notes

1.   How much of Sweden's success is dependent on its size—a population of only 9 million individuals? Can a national system of non-profit residential leasehold organizations work in the United States?

2.   Sweden's housing policies are founded on a national consensus regarding the importance of integration, justice, and equality in housing. There is a determined national effort to prevent citizens from being divided into different groups on the basis of income or other socio-economic factors. Does America's more diverse society have the same commitment or share the same goals?

3.   Despite Professor Kenn's article, Sweden continues to face a wealth of challenges to its housing goals. In recent years, new housing production has been low and a major shortage of housing is developing. Confronted with these problems, the government has formed several task forces, forums, and housing boards to address needed restructuring.

Chapter 8

EVICTION OF TENANTS

In the United States, the majority view is that a residential landlord may terminate a periodic tenancy for any reason, absent discrimination or improper retaliation. Similarly, a landlord has no obligation to renew a term of years tenancy once it expires. However, many countries impose greater restrictions on a landlord's ability to evict a residential tenant; this approach reflects a different view of the landlord-tenant relationship, which places more weight on protecting the tenant's right to housing, as discussed in Chapter 7. In most European nations, for example, a residential lease has an indefinite duration and may even be inherited by the tenant's heirs. Under this approach, a landlord must have good cause to terminate the tenancy. The two decisions below from the European Court of Human Rights discuss this issue under the laws of Portugal and Poland.

A. EVICTION IN PORTUGAL

VELOSA BARRETO v. PORTUGAL

European Court of Human Rights
Eur. Ct. H.R. 18072/91 (1995)

RYSSDAL, MACDONALD, DE MEYER, LOIZOU, BIGI, LOPES ROCHA, WILDHABER, and JAMBREK, JUDGES.

[Plaintiffs Velosa Barreto and his wife had one child. The family lived together with the wife's parents, in a house the parents had rented in Funchal, Portugal. The house had four bedrooms, a kitchen, a living-dining room, and a basement. One of the wife's brothers and two of her aunts also lived in the house from time to time. Velosa Barreto then inherited title to another house in Funchal, which had been previously rented to tenants. Plaintiffs sued to terminate that lease so that they could occupy that property

69

as their home. However, the trial court held that plaintiffs had failed to establish a true need to live in that house, because they could continue living with the wife's parents: "[T]he real need required by case-law does not exist, nor is this a case in which it is absolutely necessary or essential for the plaintiffs to recover possession of the accommodation."]

16.   The following is a translation of the main provisions of the Civil Code [of Portugal] applicable at the material time to the termination of tenancy contracts on residential property:

Article 1095: ... A landlord shall not have the right to terminate a [tenancy] contract, which shall be tacitly renewed unless terminated by the tenant in accordance with Article 1055.

Article 1096: 1. A landlord may seek termination of a [tenancy] contract on its expiry in the following cases: (a) when he needs the property in order to live there or build his home there; ...

17.   According to established case-law...a landlord's right to terminate a lease in order to occupy the property as his home may be exercised only when...the condition laid down in Article 1096(1)(a), namely the landlord's real need to live in the property, has been satisfied....

21.   Mr. Velosa Barreto alleged that the Portuguese courts, by not allowing him to terminate the lease on the house he owned, had infringed his right to respect for his private and family life. He relied on Article 8 of the Convention [for the Protection of Human Rights and Fundamental Freedoms], which provides:

1.   Everyone has the right to respect for his private and family life, his home and his correspondence.

2.   There shall be no interference by a public authority with the exercise of this right except such as is in accordance with the law and is necessary in a democratic society in the interests of national security, public safety or the economic well-being of the country, for the prevention of disorder or crime, for the protection of health or morals, or for the protection of the rights and freedoms of others.

The applicant claimed that it was implicit in Article 8 that each family had the right to a home for themselves alone. He complained in particular of the obstacles that had been placed in the way of his pursuit of a satisfactory private and family life.... His child had never had the advantage of growing up in complete privacy with his parents, and had remained an only child because of the cramped living conditions....

24.   The Court recognises that the decisions complained of prevented Mr. Velosa Barreto from living in his house, as he intended. Nevertheless, effective protection of respect for private and family

life cannot require the existence in national law of legal protection enabling each family to have a home for themselves alone. It does not go so far as to place the State under an obligation to give a landlord the right to recover possession of a rented house on request and in any circumstances.

25.   ...[T]he Court considers that the legislation applied in this case pursues a legitimate aim, namely the social protection of tenants, and that it thus tends to promote the economic well-being of the country and the protection of the rights of others.

26.   It is not in dispute that, in pursuit of those aims, the Portuguese legislature was entitled to make termination of a lease subject to the condition that the landlord "needs the property in order to live there." The only point at issue is whether, in applying the above rule to the applicant's case, the Portuguese courts infringed his right to respect for his private and family life.

27.   Mr. Velosa Barreto asserted that the Portuguese authorities had not endeavored to strike a balance between the general interest and his own interests. The assessment of need had been based solely on the fact that he lived with his parents-in-law, whose house had been adjudged large enough to accommodate his family. The judge had thus ignored the precarious and unstable situation, whose continuation depended on the goodwill and hospitality of others. . . .

28.   According to the Government, a balancing exercise between the respective interests is carried out by the courts. Determination of the existence of "need" lay entirely within the national authorities' margin of appreciation, and they had settled the dispute in accordance with criteria established by case-law and based on the principle of proportionality, the good faith of the judiciary and the social consensus. The Portuguese courts, who had direct knowledge of the relevant circumstances, were clearly better placed than the European Court to assess the facts at a given time and place.

29.   The Court notes that the Funchal Court of First Instance and the Lisbon Court of Appeal held that in the circumstances of the case existence of the "need" required by law had not been proved. Each of those courts reached that conclusion after duly considering the various questions of fact and of law submitted to it. . . . In particular, both courts took account of the fact that Mr. Velosa Barreto's situation had improved during the proceedings, since two of his wife's aunts and her brother had in the meantime left the house he was living in, leaving more room for his own household.

30.   It has not been shown. . .that by ruling as they did the Portuguese courts acted arbitrarily or unreasonably or failed to discharge their obligation to strike a fair balance between the respective interests. . . .

GOTCHEV, JUDGE (dissenting).

1. With regard to Article 8, in my view the possibility for the applicant and his family to occupy living space separate from the rooms or space where his wife's parents live is a substantive element of family life within the meaning of Article 8 of the Convention.... So the question of how many rooms there are in the parents' house and how many individuals live there is not of decisive importance for the question of family life. Both domestic courts refused to give the applicant the opportunity to live with his family in normal conditions independently from other persons who were not members of his family. Moreover, the applicant and his wife were young enough at the time of the alleged violation to have more children. Unfortunately, the Court did not attach sufficient weight to this aspect of the case. I think that the possibility of increasing the size of one's family should be regarded as one element of family life. ...

Notes

1. The Portuguese Civil Code provides that a residential lease continues to exist over time unless the landlord has good cause to terminate it. How does this view of the landlord-tenant relationship differ from the prevailing view in the United States? In particular, what does it mean to "own" a home if the owner does not have the right to live there?

2. What are the arguments for and against a requirement that a residential landlord have "good cause" to evict a tenant?

3. Does the majority opinion strike the right balance between the rights of landlords and tenants? Or should the Court have given more weight to the applicant's interest in having more children, as the dissent suggests?

4. Is it reasonable to infer that there was a shortage of affordable rental housing in Portugal at the time of this case? If so, then the tenants might have had trouble finding replacement housing. How important was this in the outcome of the case?

5. Exactly why did Velosa Barreto lose? After this case, what facts would a landlord have to prove in order to establish that he needed the property to live in?

B. EVICTION IN POLAND

HUTTEN-CZAPSKA v. POLAND

European Court of Human Rights
Eur. Ct. H.R. 35014/97 (2005)

BRATZA, PELLONPAA, STRAZNICKA, CASADEVALL, MA-RUSTE, PAVLOVSCHI and BORREGO BORREGO, JUDGES.

1. The case originated in an application...against the Republic of Poland lodged with the European Commission on Human

Rights...by Mrs. Maria Hutten–Czapska, who is a French national of Polish origin....

3. The applicant alleged, in particular, that the situation created by the implementation of the law imposing on landlords restrictions in respect of increasing rent and terminating leases that originated in administrative decisions amounted to a violation of Art. 1 of Protocol No. 1 to the Convention [for the Protection of Human Rights and Fundamental Freedoms]....

[Hutten–Czapska's parents owned a house in Gdynia, Poland. In 1945, the city ordered them to leave the house and, over time, divided the house into four apartments and permitted various tenants to live there with rent control protection. As tenants died, their relatives inherited the right to lease the apartments. In 1990, a local court declared that Hutten–Czapska had inherited the house. However, the rental income from the house was lower than the cost of maintaining it. The evidence showed that, on average, the level of controlled rent in Poland amounted to only 40% of the costs to maintain residential buildings. She filed various lawsuits and administrative proceedings under Polish law in order to evict the tenants, but without success, because she was unable to provide replacement housing for them.]

91. Section 11 of the 2001 Act listed situations in which a landlord could terminate a lease agreement that originated in an administrative decision. Section 11 (1)-(2) read, in so far as relevant:

1. If a tenant is entitled to use a dwelling for rent, the landlord may give notice [of termination] only for reasons listed in this provision....

2. The landlord may give one month's notice effective at the end of a calendar month, if:

(1) the tenant, despite a reminder in writing, still uses the dwelling in a manner contrary to the terms of the agreement or in a manner inconsistent with its function, thus causing damage; or if he or she has damaged equipment designed for common use of residents; or if he or she has flagrantly or repeatedly disturbed order, thus severely upsetting the use of other dwellings; or

(2) the tenant has fallen into more than three months' arrears of rent or other charges for the use of the dwelling and [despite notice]....has not paid those amounts; or

(3) the tenant has sublet the flat or part of it, or allowed it, or part of it, to be used free of charge by another without the landlord's authorisation; or

(4) the tenant uses the flat which has to be vacated in view of the impending demolition or substantial renovation of the building. . . .

92. Pursuant to Section 11(3), a landlord who received rent which was lower than 3% of the reconstruction value of the dwelling could terminate the agreement if a tenant had not lived in the flat for more than 12 months or if he had title to another flat situated in the same town.

Section 11(4) provided that a landlord could terminate the agreement with 6 months' notice if he intended to dwell in his own flat and had provided the tenant with "substitute accommodation" or the tenant was entitled to a dwelling which met conditions for "substitute accommodation."

Under Section 11(5), a landlord could terminate the agreement upon 3 years notice if he intended to dwell in his flat but had not provided the tenant with any "substitute accommodation." . . .

99. Article 691 of the Civil Code provides, in so far as relevant:

> In the event of a tenant's death, the following persons shall succeed to the tenancy agreement: his or her spouse if the latter has not been a party to that agreement, his or her children, his or her spouse's children, any other persons to whom he was obligated to pay maintenance, and a person living with the tenant in de facto marital cohabitation. . . .

143. The applicant considered that the impugned restrictions had gone beyond what could be considered mere "control of the use of property" and that their continued application for many years had resulted in essential elements of her right of property being practically extinguished. In fact, she was an owner only "on paper". She did not have the possibility to decide who would live in her house and for how long. The lease of flats had been imposed on her by unlawful administrative decisions but, despite that fact, she could not terminate the lease agreements and regain possession of her house because the statutory conditions attached to the termination of leases, including the duty to provide a tenant with substitute accommodation, made it impossible in practice to do so. She had no influence whatsoever on the amount of rent paid by her tenants. Indeed, under the contested laws the levels of rent were fixed without any reasonable relationship to the costs of maintaining property in good condition, which had resulted in a significant depreciation in the value and condition of her house. In her submission, the cumulative effect of all those factors had brought about a situation similar to expropriation.

144. The Government disagreed. They stressed that the applicant had never lost her right to the "peaceful enjoyment" of her proper-

ty. Since 25 October 1990, when the Gdynia District Court had entered her title in the relevant land register, she had enjoyed all the attributes of a property owner. She had a right to use, to dispose of, to pledge, to lend and even to destroy her property. The adopted measures...only amounted to the control of the use of the applicant's property.

145.   The Court notes that the applicant never lost the right to sell her property. Nor did the authorities apply any measures resulting in the transfer of her ownership. It is true that she could not exercise her right of use in terms of physical possession as the house was occupied by the tenants and that her rights in respect of letting the flats, including her right to receive rent and to terminate leases, were subject to a number of statutory limitations. However, these issues concern the degree of the State's interference, and not its nature. All the measures taken...constituted a means of State control of the use of her property. ...

150.   Not only must an interference with the right of property pursue, on the facts as well as in principle, a "legitimate aim" in the "general interest", but there must also be a reasonable relation of proportionality between the means employed and the aim sought to be realised by any measures applied by the State, including measures designed to control the use of the individual's property. That requirement is expressed by the notion of a "fair balance" that must be struck between the demands of the general interest of the community and the requirements of the protection of the individual's fundamental rights. ...

163.   [Hutten–Czapska argued that the tenancy] had been imposed on her, as it had been on other private landlords, by a unilateral decision of the State. That decision had been accompanied by severe limitations on the termination of leases. Further provisions of [the law] had set the rent chargeable at low levels, well below the average costs of maintenance of property and...had obliged the landlords to carry out costly maintenance works. That state of affairs had not improved under the 2001 Act, which had practically maintained all restrictions on termination of leases and obligations in respect of maintenance of property and which had aggravated the landlords' situation by freezing rents at unacceptably low levels.

164.   The applicant concluded by stating that the fundamental question in this case was who, and to what extent, was to bear the burden of the housing policy—landlords or the State. In her view, even the poor state of the country's budget and the costs of political and economic transformation of the State could not justify placing the main burden of making sacrifices for society's benefit on a specific group of property owners.

165. The Government considered that the authorities had maintained a reasonable relationship of proportionality between the means employed and the aims they had sought to achieve. ...

188.   Having regard to all the foregoing circumstances... the Court holds that the authorities imposed a disproportionate and excessive burden on [the applicant], which cannot be justified by any legitimate interest of the community pursued by them. There has accordingly been a violation of Art. 1 of Protocol No. 1.

Notes

1.   Why did Hutten–Czapska win? Is the Court's ruling based on the rent provisions, the restrictions on lease termination, or both? In his partly concurring and partly dissenting opinion, Judge Pavlovschi suggests that the Court "did not consider the second part of the applicant's complaint, namely that she was unable to regain her possessions or to use them."

2.   Hutten–Czapska claimed that she was the owner of the home "only on paper." What did she mean? Was she correct?

3.   Assuming that "good cause" eviction is a desirable test, should a landlord who has good cause to evict also be required to find replacement housing for the tenant?

4.   In effect, Polish law provides that (a) a residential tenancy can be terminated only for just cause and (b) such a tenancy can be inherited by family members. How long might such a tenancy exist? Is it akin to the now-obsolete defeasible fee tail?

5.   Who should bear the burden of providing housing for the poor—private landlords, the government, or someone else?

C.   THE INTERNATIONAL PERSPECTIVE

Some suggest that there is a growing international consensus against evictions without good cause. The International Covenant on Economic, Social and Cultural Rights—which binds over 140 nations (but not the United States)—recognizes "the right of everyone to an adequate standard of living for himself and his family, including adequate food, clothing and housing..." (Article 11[1]). This language is widely viewed as recognizing a human right to adequate housing. General Comment No. 7 to the Covenant, excerpted below, addresses the issue of eviction.

INTERNATIONAL COVENANT ON ECONOMIC, SOCIAL AND CULTURAL RIGHTS, GENERAL COMMENT NO. 7

(1997)

1.   In its General Comment No. 4 (1991), the Committee [which monitors implementation of the Covenant] observed that all per-

sons should possess a degree of security of tenure which guarantees legal protection against forced eviction, harassment and other threats. It concluded that forced evictions are *prima facie* incompatible with the requirements of the Covenant.... [T]he Committee is now in a position to seek to provide further clarification as to the implications of such practices in terms of the obligations contained in the Covenant.

2. The international community has long recognized that the issue of forced evictions is a serious one.... Agenda 21 stated that "people should be protected by law against unfair eviction from their homes or land." In the Habitat Agenda, governments committed themselves to "protecting all people from, and providing legal protection and redress for, forced evictions that are contrary to the law, taking human rights into consideration..." The Commission on Human Rights has also indicated that "forced evictions are a gross violation of human rights." However, [these statements] leave open one of the most critical issues, namely that of determining the circumstances under which forced evictions are permissible....

8. ...The State itself must refrain from forced evictions and ensure that the law is enforced against its agents or third parties who carry out forced evictions.... Moreover, this approach is reinforced by article 17.1 of the International Covenant on Civil and Political Rights which complements the right not to be forcefully evicted without adequate protection. That provision recognizes, *inter alia,* the right to be protected against "arbitrary or unlawful interference" with one's home....

11. Whereas some evictions may be justifiable, such as in the case of persistent non-payment of rent or of damage to rented property without any reasonable cause, it is incumbent upon the relevant authorities to ensure that they are carried out in a manner warranted by a law which is compatible with the Covenant....

Note

Paragraph 11 states that evictions for good cause "may be justifiable." Does this mean that an eviction made without good cause is a violation of the human right to adequate housing?

Chapter 9

SQUATTERS' RIGHTS AND ADVERSE POSSESSION

Much of the world's population lives on land held by informal title. Squatters often occupy property with the expectation that their possession will eventually become ownership. As described in the following passages, there is danger in squatting. Despite the hardships involved, the desire to own land—particularly land that may be inherited by one's descendants—is frequently a factor that motivates squatting. The human, social, and economic costs of squatting are high. Nations have sought various ways to remedy the underlying causes of squatting, but with little success. Poverty, internal displacement for economic or political reasons, and a lack of agricultural assistance and governmental infrastructure all lead to the practice.

Some countries have tried to address squatting directly. One method of transforming the informal title of the squatter into a legally-recognized, formal title is through adverse possession.

A. SQUATTER NARRATIVES

Roy H. May, Jr.
I Am Conchita, the Squatter

The Poor of Land: A Christian Case for Land Reform 1–3 (1991)

Between 1985 and early 1989, the Pavones de Golfito region in southern Costa Rica, on the Pacific Coast, was the scene of intense conflict among peasant squatters, North American landowners, and the Rural Assistance Guard. This is the testimony of one of the squatters.

My name is Concepción Rosales, but since I was little I've been called "Conchita." I am 32 years old; I'm the mother of six children

78

and I'm pregnant. I'm a peasant born in Guanacaste (in northern Costa Rica) and since two years ago I'm a squatter in Pavones de Golfito.

I was born in Nandayure. Later my dad went to work for the banana company [United Brands], and so we all went to Golfito; he was the only one of us working. When he died my family and I went to Punta Zancudo. I was 14 and so I began working the land. Since then that's my world.

When I was 15, I met Luís Angel Porras and married him. His family was from Pavones. We left Zancudo for Pueblo Nuevo de Coto, and then to Pavones. We worked on the farm of Alejandro Gómez, and bought a piece of land.

My husband went to pan gold at Puerto Jiménez and one day, five years ago, a tree fell on him and a companion, killing them both. I couldn't see him because he had been dead three days before I was told.

My older son, Mainor, was 14 and didn't want to stay on our little farm. We sold what we had in La Hierba de Pavones and went near the beach.

I was happy with my husband but now I was left alone. I decided to fight for a piece of land for my children and become a squatter; since then I've been thrown off the land, mistreated, and I've been in jail.

The first time that the Rural Assistance Guard came to my little house I was scared, because I'd never been in these things. But as time went by, I became accustomed to it all. Now I'm not afraid of them even though they burn my little house and destroy what I've planted. I'm not afraid now because the hope of having a little piece of land for my children and me gives me strength.

They've thrown me off seven times. The only time I was saved in these two years was in April of last year.

Now last December 9, the Guard came and I was with my companion (I started living with him a year-and-a-half ago), and was with my children. I cried more for the hunger they would feel if they were carried off, than for me. I know what it means to be in jail.

They took us that Friday and it wasn't until Saturday night they gave us something to eat. They took us from Golfito to San Isidro and again to Golfito. They sent me to the Buen Pastor Jail, and I got out today.

For me, jail has been hard because I don't know anything about my children. I believe they are with my sister-in-law who lives in Pavones. When I've been detained, I've been treated good and bad. Don Beita, of the Golfito police, doesn't let me make telephone calls and so I don't know anything about my children.

In Buen Pastor Jail, the girls behave themselves well, but I feel sorry for the little guilas ("kids"). I have six children: Mainor, 17, Meylin, who's going to be 15, Amixia, 12, Luis Iván, 10, Ana Doris, 8, and Jenny Luisa who's almost 5.

In Golfito the government agency for children has told me that if I continue being a squatter, they'll take my little kids, and that I'll never see them again, and that they'll send me to Buen Pastor Jail. That worries me, but I keep going. I want a piece of land and even though a lot of people tell me to get off, they're not going to give me or my children anything to eat.

Those of us here at Pavones are going to keep on; the struggle ends when the Lobo family and others leave us the land that they don't cultivate. My ambition is to have land even if it's just a little plot to leave to my children. It's better to live in the country than here in the city.

Kenneth L. Karst
Rights in Land and Housing in an Informal Legal System: The Barrios of Caracas

19 Am. J. Comp. L. 550, 560 (1971)

The motivating force for the move usually is the opportunity to own a home. One barrio resident spoke of his decision to move to the barrio during the early days of the barrio's formation: "I used to come by here every day. Everyone's ambition is to live under his own roof, not in an apartment that belongs to someone else. You have to ask permission for everything—to bring up a bed, to change a plug. Besides, I want to have something to leave to the children, a little house or something like that." The consideration to move to a particular barrio is importantly influenced by the presence in the barrio of relatives. That consideration far outranks others, such as convenience to employment or schools or shopping.

Notes

1. The passage above quotes a squatter living in a barrio in Caracas, Venezuela, in the mid–1960s. As part of the Law and Development Movement in the late 1960s and early 1970s, Professor Karst studied and wrote about real property ownership in Caracas. His study introduces us to the variety of barrios in and around the city, and the wide range of public services and improvements they provide. Indeed, even in the mid–1960s, many residents of barrios had some systems of

electricity, water, and sewage. The unofficial governing juntas of barrios recognized the ownership of land and houses, and settled questions of boundary disputes, easements, and nuisance law. Most occupants thought that when faced with a claim by a "true owner," the occupant would be able to reach an agreement to stay on the land. The true owner of the land in the Venezuelan context was frequently the state which, by providing electricity, water, and other services, eroded its claim to have the property vacated. Over time, occupants improved their houses; on the floor, cement replaced dirt; for walls, block replaced temporary walls. Although few homeowners had documents establishing their ownership of the property, as Karst notes, "this steady accretion of housing investment—what a young Venezuelan sociologist called 'a work of ants'—demonstrates beyond doubt that the barrio residents feel secure in the occupancy of their houses." Karst, *supra* at 569.

2. Does it appear from the readings that squatting is purely a product of poverty? If not, what other factors are relevant?

3. What does a squatter own? What mechanisms serve to enforce informal title?

B. FROM INFORMAL TITLE TO FORMAL TITLE THROUGH ADVERSE POSSESSION

Winter King
Illegal Settlements and the Impact of Titling Programs

44 Harv. Int'l L.J. 433, 433–34, 439–41, 448–56, 470–71 (2003)

Driving outward from the center of Lima, Peru, one witnesses, in reverse, the development of informal settlements, known as *pueblos jovenes*, that encircle the city. Lima is located on a desert coast—one of the driest in the world—made up of large hills of sand. These are the foothills of the Andes. While once these hills were bare, now they support thousands of small homes. The first of these settlements grew adjacent to the old city of Lima and has now existed for decades. During this time, the inhabitants have improved their homes and provided infrastructure, transforming the former "shanty-towns" into nearly middle-class suburbs. As one drives further outward, the settlements are younger and less developed: unfinished one-story structures have replaced two-story cement houses a few miles out; on the very edges, there are only straw mat huts, clinging to the hillsides, and the occasional private water truck, delivering potable water to the inhabitants. There are no paved roads or sewage lines.

What the casual driver cannot see or know by simply observing these settlements is that the settlers do not possess title to their lands. Most have constructed their homes in the course of an "invasion"—a term used for a mass, organized squatting typically on public, but sometimes on private, land. Others have "encroached" on private or public land, setting up their shacks on land adjacent to the land owned by a family member or friend. Some have actually purchased their plots, but have bought them as illegal subdivisions of larger, titled property. In either case, the settlers are trespassers, and may be evicted from their plots by the true owner at any time.

These developments by no means constitute a small portion of housing in Lima, or in any other city in the majority world. According to one estimate, eighty-five percent of urban dwellings in these countries are informal—that is, they "(i) were built in violation of express laws, (ii) did not comply with requirements for access to land, (iii) were originally formal but became informal, or (iv) were built by the government without complying with legal requirements." The consequences of this huge informal housing sector range from technical, bureaucratic difficulties to concrete health problems, like cholera or dengue fever, caused by a lack of adequate water and sewage treatment. Historically, these developments have been either ignored or destroyed by the government. However, as states have realized that persistent rural-urban migration has converted these informal settlements into permanent additions to their metropolitan areas, they have attempted to solve some of the problems that both cause and accompany illegal development.

This Article analyzes three ways that states have attempted to deal with informal, irregular, or illegal settlements. While the ultimate goal of each is to bring all land development into the legal fold, the methods vary greatly in their means and policy effects. The first method invokes the legal principle of adverse possession. Here, squatters must demonstrate that they have occupied their lands for a certain amount of time, and in some cases must also show that they have improved the land or put it to use....

A number of scholars have addressed the dangers—both physical and social—that illegal settlements pose for those who live in them, as well as for the society at large. According to some scholars, these self-built settlements provide the solution to the extreme low-income housing shortage in the majority world. Studies of these areas indicate that they actually provide a kind of upward mobility for the poor. For a very small, up-front investment, inhabitants gain access to property that would, if purchased formally, be prohibitively expensive....

[W]hile one might applaud the ingenuity and resourcefulness of the settlers, one must also recognize the extreme risks they take—risks that not only endanger themselves, but also society at large. These risks can be divided into two classes: physical and social. . . .

Most states have followed one of three models in attempting to reduce the problems that both cause and result from illegal settlements. First, a state might adhere to an adverse possession model, in which title is granted to illegal settlers after they have resided on the property for a certain amount of time and have acted in ways (also specified) that signal that they are claiming the land as their own. Alternatively, a state that adopts the ad hoc/political model will grant titles to illegal settlers in an ad hoc fashion, usually motivated by some political exigency or as an attempt to garner political support. The final policy adoption available to states is the state-as-developer model, in which the state purchases land (or uses public property), provides minimal but necessary infrastructure, and sells the developed property back to would-be illegal settlers at cost. . . .

A.   The Adverse Possession Model

According to Anglo–American common law, adverse possession provides a statute of limitations "fixing the period of time beyond which the owner of land can no longer bring an action, or undertake self-help, for the recovery of his land from a person in possession of the land." Not all possession is allowed to ripen into title, however. Adverse possession requires "that the possession be (1) actual, (2) open and notorious, (3) exclusive, (4) continuous, and (5) hostile under a claim of right." Thus, if an individual possesses land in this way for the statutorily prescribed amount of time, the title of the land will be transferred from the former true owner to the adverse possessor.

The law of adverse possession is found in the law of a number of majority world countries. In Brazil, for example, it is called *usucapiao*, and it formerly "required a pacific permanence on the land for as long a time as twenty years in most cases." In Peru, the name given this rule is *prescripcion adquisitiva*, which similarly requires "continuous, pacific and public (as if the possessor were the true owner) possession during ten years. It is acquired in five years when the possessor has colorable title and good faith."

One interesting and. . .important distinction between the requirements of American adverse possession and either *usucapiao* or *prescripcion adquisitiva* is that the latter two can be used against vacant government land. Only "assets of public use," like schools, streets, roads, public squares, canals, and bridges, are immune from acquisition by this method. Thus, if a piece of government land is settled and occupied pacifically, *prescripcion adquisitiva* could be used by settlers to gain title to their property. . . .

Peru has also established an adverse possession-based law for title acquisition outside of its general *prescripcion adquisitiva*. Through the Formalization Commission of Informal Property (CO-FOPRI), the state will grant title under the following conditions: (1) the land occupied must have been national, public, or municipal since before 1996; and (2) the possessor must have documents guaranteeing that the land has been publicly and pacifically possessed for a period not less than one year. Some examples of such guaranteeing documents include marriage or birth certificates on which appears the address of the property claimed, a receipt from a purchase that includes the address, and private documents transferring possession to the current occupant from the earlier one. While one year is a relatively short amount of time for providing notice to the true owner or other possible claimants, the invasions of property in Peru are generally of such a size that they receive local if not national news coverage, which serves as an additional source of notice.

While this program only applies to informal settlements on public lands, COFOPRI also "provides the mechanisms for negotiation, expropriation, and *prescripcion adquisitiva*" in cases where settlements are on private lands. Thus, the general rule of adverse possession is used in cases of private land—meaning that the occupier must show they have lived on the property for at least ten years and have occupied it "like the owner himself."

B. The Consequences of the Adverse Possession Model

. . .First, the adverse possession model does little to prevent danger associated with violent invasion. The adverse possessor must still invade property and maintain her stake in it for a period of time. During that time, she must not only defend against eviction by the true owner, but also must defend against other invaders' claims. Precisely because they do not have the force of the law to keep trespassers or usurpers off of "their" property, settlers must resort to individual force. However, where the adverse possession model also incorporates a requirement that possession be pacific, as in the general *usucapiao* and *prescripcion adquisitiva* laws in Brazil and Peru, invaders may be deterred from occupying lands that could result in a violent confrontation. . . .

Second, adverse possession-based legislation may be tailored to influence the kind of terrain on which invasions take place. . . . The adverse possession model might be flexible enough to include within it a limitation on where adverse possession can take place. Just as legislation can remove public assets or state-owned property from the pool of available, invadable land, so too could it exclude property that is not safe for human habitation. . . .

Adverse possession only addresses the issue of public health and the provision of services indirectly. . . . It is important to note that while some upgrading can be put off safely (e.g., a second story, possibly electricity), sewage treatment and disposal as well as safe drinking water are necessities from the beginning of a settlement. Thus, even a relatively short statute of limitations, if it hinders provision of these services, could pose serious health risks to the population. . . .

Turning to the social problems of illegality, adverse possession legalizes the claims of those who possess property in illegal settlements, transferring ownership rights from the "true owner" to the adverse possessor. While, as shown above, adverse possession-based methods of state governance do not adequately solve all the physical problems of the settlements, they do solve the social problems that are more directly tied to the fact of the settlements' illegality.

Because the adverse possession method effectively formalizes the once illegal settler's ownership of her land (albeit only after a period of waiting), it may adequately resolve the economic problems found in illegal settlements. De Soto's concern—that illegal property equals dead capital—is similarly addressed by adverse possession. Transaction costs are also lowered through adverse possession: after title is granted, the property is easier to sell or rent. . . . Thus, economic concerns are addressed comprehensively by the adverse possession model.

With respect to the rule-of-law-related problems, the adverse possession model alleviates some of the concerns identified above. While it remains true that a regime of adverse possession rewards the illegal behavior of a trespasser, the basic rule of adverse possession has existed in many of these countries for some time, and is accompanied by clear rules and processes required before any transfer of rights can take place. . . .

This concern leads us to the next problem identified with illegal settlements: whatever method is chosen, it should not encourage more illegal settlements. In the context of the adverse possession model, the encouragement of more illegal settlements would likely constitute the proliferation and expansion of settlement attempts in the wake of such a regime's introduction or liberalization. . . .

However, adverse possession need not be seen as an on-off switch, applying to all comers equally. As with programs in Peru and Brazil that limit their scope to public lands, its requirements can be tailored to serve certain policy objectives. In this context, to discourage illegal settlement would be to nip somehow a would-be settler's incentive to attempt an adverse possession in the bud, perhaps via regulation. . . .

While the adverse possession regime is likely to encourage illegal conduct in the short term, an alternative perspective would counter that the regime actually discourages illegal conduct by drawing more low-income persons into the formal property sector in the long term. . . .

Finally, the adverse possession model offers the state a low-cost, economically viable solution to the problem of low-income housing shortage. If many of the illegal settlements occur on state-owned land, the state's only cost in granting title under the adverse possession model is the cost associated with not developing the land in an alternative manner (e.g., exploitation of natural resources; sale to buyers who can afford to pay; development of other urban infrastructure, such as roads, hospitals, or schools). If the settlements occur on private lands, there is even less actual cost to the state, as the lost value of the land is paid for by the individual private landowner. . . .

In sum, the titling method of adverse possession provides settlers with some protection from the economic and social dangers of illegal settlements. It also offers the state a relatively low-cost method of regularization. It may, nevertheless, encourage future illegal settlements by holding out the possibility of gaining title at some time in the not-too-distant future. It also does little to cure the problems associated with the initial violence of invasion. . . .

Illegal settlements have proved to be a puzzling fact of contemporary life in most majority world cities. While first viewed as slums, to be demolished or relocated, they have come to be considered as a solution to low-cost housing shortages, and even markers of the latent wealth of the poor. However, there are numerous costs and risks associated with living in the informal property sector. . . .

With nearly eighty-five percent of majority world citizens occupying property illegally, any increase in legal ownership and the installation of public services would move these citizens and their countries toward successful capitalism, and, perhaps more importantly, into healthier, safer, homes.

Notes

1. How does the narrative of Conchita Rosales illustrate the concerns raised by Winter King?

2. Why do Brazil and Peru permit adverse possession against vacant government lands, while the United States generally prohibits this practice? Does the increase in homelessness in the United States suggest that we should reconsider this prohibition?

3.   What is the origin of the adverse possession doctrine? Is the use of adverse possession to give legal title to squatters a proper extension of the doctrine? Does your answer differ for the United States and for Latin American countries? If so, why?

4.   What is the relationship between squatting and poverty? Between squatting and national economic development? Between squatting and affordable housing?

Chapter 10

THE RIGHT TO EXCLUDE

A landowner in the United States has a broad right to exclude any other person from her land. Indeed, the Supreme Court has characterized the right to exclude as "one of the most essential sticks in the bundle of rights that are commonly called property." *Kaiser Aetna v. United States*, 444 U.S. 164, 176 (1979). We inherited our absolutist view of the right to exclude—together with most of our property law—from England in the 1700s. Ironically, England has recently moved away from this rigid view, by restricting the right of rural landowners to exclude recreational hikers. A parallel situation arose in France, where a new statute prevented rural landowners from excluding hunters. Both developments are discussed below.

A. EXCLUDING HIKERS IN ENGLAND

Historically, most agricultural land in England was farmed on a communal basis; as a result, fields were unfenced and people could walk freely through open, uncultivated lands. Peasants often held certain traditional rights on such lands, such as the ability to take wood for fuel or to raise livestock. During the sixteenth century, however, changing economic and social conditions led to the "enclosure movement," whereby these common lands were split into separate parcels held in fee simple absolute. As part of this process, rights that peasants had traditionally enjoyed in common lands were terminated. Thus, the law recognized the absolute right of the fee simple owner to exclude everyone else from his land, as the excerpt below from Sir William Blackstone's famous treatise reflects.

The enclosure movement was highly unpopular. Yet by the nineteenth century, when Parliament finally took effective steps to regulate enclosures, almost all common land had already been enclosed. Beginning in 1880, a series of bills was introduced in

Parliament to create a statutory right to wander over open lands—such as moorland, heaths, and mountains—but without success. Pressure for reform continued, sometimes evidenced by demonstrations where mass trespassing occurred.

The Labour Party Manifesto of 1997 pledged "greater freedom for people to explore our open countryside." Thus, in 1998, the newly-elected Labour government began a consultation process which eventually culminated in the Countryside and Rights of Way Act, adopted by Parliament in 2000. This Act creates a new statutory right of pedestrian access to about 4,000,000 acres of open, undeveloped land—covering approximately 10% of England and Wales. For instance, the West Yorkshire downs made famous in *Wuthering Heights*—long closed to the public—can now be visited by hikers. Excerpts from the Act, and the debates that led up to it, are set forth below.

Sir William Blackstone
Commentaries on the Laws of England

Book III, 209–210 (1768)

...Every unwarrantable entry on another's soil the law entitles a trespass by *breaking his close*; ... For every man's land is in the eye of the law, inclosed and set apart from his neighbor's: and that either by a visible and material fence, as one field is divided from another by a hedge; or, by an ideal invisible boundary, existing only in the contemplation of law, as when one man's land adjoins to another's in the same field. Every such entry or breach of a man's close carries necessarily along with it some damage or other: for, if no other special loss can be assigned, yet still the words of the writ itself specify one general damage, *viz.* the treading down and bruising his herbage.

Countryside and Rights of Way Act

2000, c. 37 (Eng.)

Be it enacted by the Queen's most Excellent Majesty, by and with the advice and consent of the Lords Spiritual and Temporal, and Commons, in this present Parliament assembled, and by the authority of the same, as follows: ...

1. (1) In this Part "access land" means any land which: (a) is shown as open country on a map in conclusive form issued by the appropriate countryside body for the purposes of this Part... [or] (d) is situated more than 600 metres above sea level in any area for which no such map relating to open country has been issued....

(2) In this Part..."open country" means land which (a) appears to the appropriate countryside body to consist wholly or predominantly of mountain, moor, heath or down, and (b) is not registered common land....

2. (1) Any person is entitled by virtue of this subsection to enter and remain on any access land for the purposes of open-air recreation, if and so long as (a) he does so without breaking or damaging any wall, fence, hedge, stile or gate, and (b) he observes the general restrictions in Schedule 2....

Schedule 2

1. Section 2(1) does not entitle a person to be on any land, if in or on that land, he: (a) drives or rides any motor vehicle..., (b) uses a vessel or sailboard on any non-tidal water, (c) has with him any animal other than a dog, (d) commits any criminal offence, (e) lights or tends a fire or does any act which is likely to cause a fire, (f) intentionally or recklessly takes, kills, injures or disturbs any animal, bird or fish, (g) intentionally or recklessly takes, damages or destroys any eggs or nests, (h) feeds any livestock, (i) bathes in any non-tidal water, (j) engages in any operations of or connected with hunting..., (k) uses or has with him any metal detector, (*l*) intentionally removes, damages or destroys any plant, shrub, tree or root..., (m) obstructs the flow of any drain or watercourse..., (n) without reasonable excuse, interferes with any fence, barrier or other device designed to prevent accidents to people or to enclose livestock, (o) neglects to shut any gate..., ... (r) without reasonable excuse, does anything which...disturbs, annoys or obstructs any persons engaged in a lawful activity on the land, (s) engages in any organised games, or in camping, hang-gliding or para-gliding, or (t) engages in any activity which is organised or undertaken...for any commercial purpose.

Debate in the House of Commons, March 26, 1999

328 Parl. Deb., H.C. (6th ser.) (1999) 629–93 (excerpts)

Mr. Gordon Prentice (Pendle): I beg to move, That the Bill be now read a Second time. I shall not speak for long because the Government have already spoken for me and for millions of our fellow citizens who wish to enjoy their countryside. The Government are now pledged to introduce a statutory right of area access to more than 4 million acres of some of the most beautiful countryside in England and Wales. ... A National Opinion Poll survey published recently showed that 85 per cent. of the public want a statutory right to roam, with commonsense restrictions to protect the environment, crops and animals. The Conservative party is backing the 15 per cent. of the population who think that that proposition is outrageous. We in Britain have waited more than a century for a statutory right to roam. It has been a century of struggle, with the people pitted against the land-owning interests, who want to keep the land exclusively for themselves. The countryside is not the personal fiefdom of country landowners and they had better get used to that. The Government are addressing the concerns of people living in rural areas—people who were neglected by the Conservatives.... [Our] vision is not of people in red outfits riding about with dogs, but of jobs and strong, vibrant communities in our rural areas; it is of access to transport in the countryside and of services, such as village shops. We want a living, working countryside. That vision is parodied by the Conservatives, who tell us that we are the wreckers. The land is ours; it is for all of us to share and enjoy, but the landowners want it for their exclusive use; they do not want to share it. That is why we must legislate to give people that right....

Mr. James Paice (South–East Cambridgeshire): ...The hon. Gentleman's speech...underlined the fact that the Bill and this whole proposition serve to demonstrate the divide between socialism, and capitalism and property ownership. It is a totally socialist measure. I am sure the hon. Gentleman will take that as a compliment.... The right to roam is based not on a putative enjoyment of the countryside, but on one thing and one thing alone: that most evil of human traits, envy. It is based on envy of private property and a belief that land should be available to everyone and that no one should have the right to restrict access to it.... No one has specified what can be gained from open access that could not be secured through a comprehensive network of footpaths. That should be the Government's aim: to provide opportunities for people throughout the country to enjoy a good walk in the countryside near where they live. This draconian measure will benefit a small minority, will apply only to certain parts of the country and will be of no value whatsoever to the vast majority of people....

Mr. Tom Brake (Carshalton and Wallington): I congratulate the hon. Member for Pendle (Mr. Prentice) on securing this debate and on his boisterous, knockabout speech. ... Whichever side of the argument they are on, people care passionately about the right to roam. However, the issue is not, as some Conservative Members have suggested, about class war. The right to roam is not evil, but involves fundamental freedoms. Nevertheless, the right to roam issue leaves me in a quandary. I strongly support the principle that land should be accessible to all. There is no justification for placing off limits to all but a small minority the vast tracts of our memorable countryside. ... But, on the other hand: the right to access must encompass only low or no-impact access. I believe that the Right to Roam Bill does not quite get the balance right. ...

Mr. Gareth R. Thomas (Harrow, West): ...Walking and rambling are hugely popular in this country. More than 400 million walking trips were made in 1996. A statutory right to roam will further increase the opportunities for leisure activity—for healthy walking, for tourism and for increased understanding of our environment. A statutory right to roam would build on, and increase, the opportunities available through the existing rights of way network. Above all, it would deliver huge pleasure to all those who take advantage of it. We have some stunning scenery in our nation, but enjoyment of far too much of it is denied to the many and left locked up in the hands of a privileged few.... The voluntary approach has had enough time to deliver results. The right of access to land is not an issue that has suddenly arisen. It has been a political issue for more than 100 years....

Debate in the House of Lords, May 19, 1999

601 Parl. Deb., H.L. (5th ser.) (1999) 311–21 (excerpts)

Lord Beaumont of Whitley: ...There is a general principle that almost everyone accepts, although landowners from time to time tend slightly to forget it, that individuals are not the owners of land. They hold it as stewards under the Queen, who holds it as steward under God. The rights of individual landowners are severely limited by the rights that those superior landlords hold on behalf of the community. In a way, the land of this country belongs to the people of this country. The Government are to be congratulated on their attempt to put some of that principle into practice. The right to roam is a principle, and a very good principle. But, like all principles, it needs some limitation. It is subject to the need to protect the legitimate interests of the land's occupants, among whom I include not only the stewards who hold it as landlords and the farmers who farm it, but also the wildlife that actually occupies it. ...

Earl Peel: ...I regard the proposals as one of the most savage attacks on basic property rights that has ever been seen in this country. ... I have no doubt from my own experience that the majority of walkers respect the countryside and its traditional management and do not want to compromise its well-being. Furthermore, I do not believe that the majority of walkers actually want open access and the right to roam. ... We all have a stake in the countryside, but that cannot give everyone on this small island of ours the right to decide what to do there and when. Management decisions based on experience and local knowledge must be allowed to prevail. ...

Earl Ferrers: I do not agree with the noble Lord...who said that the countryside belongs to the people. With the greatest respect to him, I think that is a whole lot of old rubbish; indeed, it belongs to the individual owners. That does not mean to say that others should not have the advantage of it and indeed access to it. But to say that it belongs to the people is simply not true. Sometimes it belongs to a smallholder, sometimes to a landowner, sometimes to a person who just has a house in a garden, sometimes to a company and sometimes to a trust. So all those different owners enjoy a certain privilege. However, they also enjoy a great responsibility....

It has been said that 80 per cent of the people who answered the consultation document were in favour of the right to roam. But if you sent out a consultation document which asked, "Would you like a free bottle of champagne?", I should think you would get quite a substantial answer in one way. The fact is that if that document had asked, "Are you in favour of people trampling over nesting birds?", a different response might have been received. The access to the countryside has to be managed. People do not walk in a straight line. Dogs will be let off the lead and they will sniff out birds and worry sheep. Moreover, people will want to brew up a cup of tea and, inadvertently, set fire to a place. Indeed, what happens when people camp at night? Who will see them off? ... Whose responsibility is it to look after [environmentally-sensitive] places? Is it to be the responsibility of the landlord? Further, what happens if he has to take out greater liability insurance? What happens if someone falls down a hole on some else's land? Who will pay for that?

Notes

1. What were the strongest arguments in favor of the "right to roam"? What were the strongest arguments against recognizing this right? As a member of Parliament, how would you have voted on the issue and why?

2. What is the practical effect of the "right to roam" on landowners? Blackstone observed that even "treading down and bruising...herbage" was a form of damage. If a hiker has the right to walk across a 1,000 acre tract of open English moorland, will this cause any real harm to the owner?

3. During the House of Lords debate, one peer told the story of finding an injured American lying on a country hillside; the American allegedly said, "Don't touch me until the ambulance comes, and who do I sue?" Do landowners have good cause to be concerned about increased liability for personal injury?

4. Lord Beaumont observed that owners hold their rights as "stewards under the Queen, who holds it as steward under God." What are the implications of this view?

5. Should the British government be required to compensate the affected landowners? Is the Countryside and Rights of Way Act truly a "socialist measure," one step in the direction of expropriating private land?

6. Now that England has abandoned Blackstone's rigid view of the right to exclude, is it time for the United States to do the same? Should we allow recreational hikers to enter open, rural land without the owner's consent?

B. EXCLUDING HUNTERS IN FRANCE

If landowners in England cannot exclude hikers, should landowners in France be able to exclude hunters?

CHASSAGNOU AND OTHERS v. FRANCE

European Court of Human Rights
29 Eur. H.R. Rep. 615, 624–26, 674–79 (1999)

WILDHABER, PALM, CAFLISCH, MAKARCZYK, KURIS, COSTA, FURHMANN, JUNGWIERT, FISCHBACH, ZUPANCIC, VAJIC, THOMASSEN, TSATSA–NIKOLOVSKA, PANTIRU, BAKA, LEVITS, and TRAJA, JUDGES.

. . .

11. Until the French Revolution of 1789 the right to hunt was a privilege of the nobility. Only nobles could take game, which was regarded as the lord's property. During the revolution there were two schools of thought on the question. The first approach, supported by Mirabeau, was to make the right to hunt the prerogative of the landowner alone; the second, which was advocated by Robespierre, was to give all citizens unconditional freedom to hunt everywhere. The first approach carried the day, as in the night of 4 August 1789 the privilege of hunting was abolished "subject to the sole reservation that landowners alone may hunt" and a decree of 11 August 1789 laid down the principle that: "Every landowner has the right to destroy or cause to be destroyed, on his property only, any species of game." Subsequently the Law of 3 May 1844...regulated the right to hunt by introducing hunting licenses and laying down fixed hunting seasons. Section 1 of that Law, which was later codified as art 365 of the Countryside Code...and then art L 222–1, provided: "No one shall have the right to hunt on land belonging to another without the consent of the owner or any person entitled through or under the owner." ...

13. It was in those circumstances that law no 64–696 of 10 July 1964, known as the Loi Verdeille, was enacted.... This provided for the creation of approved municipal hunters' associations (*associations communales de chasse agréées*—ACCAs).... Section

1...states that their object is—"to encourage, on their hunting grounds, an increase in game stocks, the destruction of vermin and the prevention of poaching...." To that end, the law requires the owners of landholdings smaller in area than a certain threshold...[20 hectares, less than roughly 50 acres] to become members of any ACCA set up in their municipality and to transfer to it the hunting rights over their lands in order to create municipal hunting grounds....

16.   Mrs. Chassagnou, Mr. Petit and Mrs. Lasgrezas...are farmers and live in the *departement* of Dordogne.... They own landholdings there smaller than 20 hectares in a single block which are included in the hunting grounds of the ACCAs of Tourtoirac and Chourgnac-d'Ans.

17.   In 1985, as members of the Anti–Hunting Movement (the ROC), and later of the Association for the Protection of Wildlife (the ASPAS), an approved association of recognised public usefulness with regard to the protection of nature, the applicants placed notices at the boundaries of their property bearing the words "Hunting prohibited" and "Sanctuary". The ACCAs...then applied for an injunction requiring the removal of these notices. The judge competent to hear urgent applications granted the injunction....

[The appeals filed by Chassagnou and the other owners within the French judicial system were ultimately unsuccessful; they applied for relief to the European Commission of Human Rights, which in turn referred the case to the European Court of Human Rights.]

72.   The applicants submitted that the obligation for them to transfer hunting rights over their land to an ACCA, against their will and without compensation or consideration, constituted an abnormal deprivation of their right to use their property [in violation of Article 1 of Protocol No. 1 to the Convention for the Protection of Human Rights and Fundamental Freedoms, reprinted in Chapter 2], firstly in that they were obliged to tolerate the presence of hunters on their land, whereas they were opposed to hunting for ethical reasons, and secondly in that they could not use the land they owned for the creation of nature preserves where hunting was prohibited.

73.   The Government, on the other hand, submitted that the interference with the applicants' right of property was minor since they had not really been deprived of their right to use their property. The Loi Verdeille had not abolished the right to hunt, which was one attribute of the right of property, but was only intended to attenuate the exclusive exercise of that right by landowners. The only thing the applicants had lost was their right to prevent other people from hunting on their land. But hunting was

practised for six months of the year and...the code expressly provided that land within a 150 metre radius of any dwelling...was not to be hunted over by ACCA members.

74.   The Court notes that, although the applicants have not been deprived of their right to use their property, to lease it or to sell it, the compulsory transfer of the hunting rights over their land to an ACCA prevents them from making use of the right to hunt, which is directly linked to the right of property, as they see fit....

75.   It is well-established case law that...an interference [with the right of property] must achieve a "fair balance" between the demands of the general interest of the community and the requirements of the protection of the individual's fundamental rights. ... [T]here must be a reasonable relationship of proportionality between the means employed and the aim pursued....

80.   The applicants asserted that the compulsory transfer of hunting rights over their land to an ACCA was a disproportionate interference with the right to the peaceful enjoyment of their possessions. They submitted that they had no means of avoiding this transfer, in spite of the applications they had made to the ACCAs or the prefects to obtain the removal of their properties from the hunting grounds of the ACCAs concerned. ...

81.   The Government rejected this argument. It submitted that the Loi Verdeille provided a broad range of means whereby landowners who wished to avoid its application could do so. They referred in that connection to the fact that it was open to the applicants to enclose their properties [with a fence]..., to acquire...additional land contiguous with their own [to create a parcel larger than 20 hectares, and thus exempt from the law], or to ask the ACCAs to include their land in the game reserve that each ACCA was required to set up.... The Government further emphasised that the owners were not compelled to transfer their hunting rights to an ACCA without receiving any consideration; they admittedly lost their exclusive right to hunt but this loss was made good by the fact that for their part they could hunt throughout the ACCA's hunting grounds. ...

82.   The Court considers that none of the options mentioned by the Government would in practice have been capable of absolving the applicants from the statutory obligation to transfer hunting rights over their land to ACCAs. It notes in particular that the fence referred to...must be continuous, unbroken and incapable of being breached by game animals or human beings, which presupposes that it must be of a certain height and strength. The applicants could not be required to incur considerable expense in order to avoid [their statutory obligation].... As to the assertion that it was open to the applicants to ask for their land to be

included in a game preserve..., the Court notes that neither the ACCAs, nor the minister nor the prefect are required to grant such requests from private individuals, as shown by the refusals of the applicants' requests in the present case.... With regard to the various forms of statutory consideration mentioned by the Government, the Court takes the view that these cannot be considered to represent fair compensation for loss of the right of use. ... [The statute] does not contemplate any measure of compensation for landowners opposed to hunting, who, by definition, do not wish to derive any advantage or profit from a right to hunt which they refuse to exercise. ...

85.   In conclusion, notwithstanding the legitimate aims of the Loi Verdeille when it was adopted, the Court considers that the result of the compulsory-transfer system which it lays down has been to place the applicants in a situation which upsets the fair balance to be struck between protection of the right of property and the requirements of the general interest. ... There has therefore been a violation...[of the Convention].

Notes

1.   Compare the "right to roam" in Britain with the "right to hunt" created by the Loi Verdeille. Which is more intrusive on the rights of owners? Which best serves the interests of the general public?

2.   In many jurisdictions in the United States, an owner must post "No Trespassing" signs on rural, unenclosed land in order to bar hunters; otherwise, hunters have an implied license to enter. *See generally* Mark R. Sigmon, Note, *Hunting and Posting on Private Land in America*, 54 Duke L.J. 549 (2004). Yet, in general, recreational hikers are not entitled to enter unposted rural land. What accounts for this difference?

3.   In light of *Chassagnou*, does the "right to roam" created by the Countryside and Rights of Way Act violate the Convention for the Protection of Human Rights and Fundamental Freedoms? In the House of Lords debate leading up to passage of the Act, Lord Brittan cited *Chassagnou* and described its holding as follows: "It is clear that the Court found that the granting of rights to people on other people's land amounted to a breach of the convention." 601 Parl. Deb., H.L. (5th ser.) (1999) 797.

4.   For centuries, Finland, Norway, and Sweden have recognized a right of public access to wild lands. In these countries, a person may roam freely over privately-owned land in the countryside, without obtaining permission from the owner. In Sweden, for example, one may travel by foot, bicycle, horse, or skis through rural lands; temporary camping is also allowed. Is this traditional right in danger after *Chassagnou*?

Chapter 11

THE LAND SALE TRANSACTION

The procedures for land sales transactions vary widely around the world. The process for selecting the property, agreeing to purchase it, assuring its quality of title, and transferring title differs from nation to nation. Examining a model from another country helps us to understand and evaluate the prevailing approach in the United States. The materials in this chapter describe a typical sale of residential property in Colombia, which uses the civil law system.

A. A LAND SALE IN COLOMBIA

1. *Finding the Property*

A standard classified advertisement for a house in the rural, bucolic neighborhood of Chia, outside Bogotá, Colombia, might read something like this:

> *Chia. Great opportunity: beautiful, gated community, four bedrooms, study, three baths, double garage, 125 square meters. Telephone: 3105554444.*

Newspaper ads are the most commonly used method of identifying a potential property for purchase in Colombia. Printed in columns underneath the names of city regions (north, south, etc.) and by sectors (neighborhoods or large developments), they are placed by owners or by real estate brokers who have exclusive listings. "For Sale" signs in windows of apartments or houses also continue to be popular, but in some areas use of such signs has declined due to concerns about criminal and fraudulent activity.

In a term coined by Germán Morales, a lawyer now practicing in Miami, another method of growing popularity for locating property in Colombia is the "Watchman Real Estate Intermediary."

Because many apartments and communities in Colombia are protected by a guarded, single-access gate, the guards—who usually hold these positions for many years—know whether any of the residents intend to sell. A prospective buyer will simply ask the guard if there is anything coming available; the guard may quickly provide a contact telephone number. It is customary to give the guard a tip or other compensation for this assistance.

Another traditional method is to use a real estate broker. Brokers are not regulated in Colombia, so no special training or licensing is required. Brokers are selected by word-of-mouth, from their telephone numbers listed on "For Sale" signs, or through a voluntary association of real estate brokers (Lonja de Propiedad Raíz) that seeks to standardize practices and to assure the public that its member brokers provide quality service.

There is no multiple-listing service or any other general compilation of listings. Real estate advertising websites do exist and will most likely gain in popularity, if not completely replace many of the other methods. Several different brokers may list the same property. Listing agreements are usually oral, and the amount of the commission is the most important term. By custom, a commission of three percent of the sales price is common in urban areas, and five percent is common in rural areas. Owners almost always have the right to sell on their own, without paying a fee to the broker who listed the property.

2. Negotiating the Agreement

After selecting a property, the buyer negotiates with the seller. Typically no written offer is sent to the seller; instead, the terms are negotiated orally. The parties usually first reach agreement on the important terms, such as price, method of payment, and execution of the Public Deed of Sale; a discussion of minor terms, such as repairs, painting, transaction costs, and deposits, then follows.

The parties next prepare and sign an Agreement of Sale, which must meet all the general requirements for a contract under Colombian Civil Code § 1611. The Agreement must include the price, method of payment, date for the execution of the Public Deed of Sale, and boundaries of the property. A provision for an earnest money deposit, which is applied to the sale price at execution of the Public Deed of Sale, or upon default, is common. If the buyer defaults, the earnest money is usually retained by the seller. If the seller defaults, the buyer is entitled to double the earnest money. Lawyers are typically not used to draft the Agreement; instead, the parties almost always use model forms, perhaps two or three pages long, which are sold in bookstores. Although illegal, the price stated on the Public Deed of Sale (the amount used for tax assessment) may be significantly less than the price listed in the Agreement of Sale.

3. *Arranging Financing*

If there is an existing mortgage on the property, the buyer will often approach the same lender, such as a bank or savings and loan association (corporación de ahorro y vivienda). A single lender is preferable for simplicity and flexibility. The lender will typically lend up to two-thirds the appraised value of the property. The lender will collect financial, identity, and title information concerning the transaction, in addition to a copy of the Agreement of Sale. After a credit analysis of the buyer, the title information will be forwarded to the lender's legal department for study. Upon determination of satisfactory title, the legal department will approve the loan and draft a mortgage agreement. The lender's determination of title for the purposes of the loan is frequently the only title work performed; the costs are borne by the lender, and the determination is not a part of the agreement or a basis for claims by the buyer in the future. Colombian Civil Code § 1915 (set forth below) lists the type of title defects the seller must cure to avoid rescission or a reduction in price.

The mortgage agreement with the bank or other lender is offered on a take-it-or-leave-it basis. Rather than being expressed in an amount of Colombian pesos, the loan may be a number of "UPACs." A "UPAC" is a Unit of Constant Power of Acquisition, a monetary unit certified by the Colombian Superintendency of Banking, which is used to avoid the effects of extreme fluctuations in currency as a result of inflation or other financial instability. Thus the peso equivalent of the principal of the loan moves up and down with the value of a UPAC, apart from the interest rate on the loan. The lender will also require proof of hazard insurance, with the lender listed as the primary beneficiary.

The mortgage agreement must be taken to the notary office where the Public Deed of Sale is to be executed. The mortgage must be registered in the Registry of Public Documents within 90 days after the Public Deed of Sale has been issued. It will be linked to the folio number of the property in the registry of real property.

4. *Executing the Deed*

With financing in place, the parties, including the lender, meet at the notary office as arranged in the Agreement of Sale. The terms of the Agreement of Sale and the mortgage are incorporated into the Public Deed of Sale. The notary calculates the notarial fee, taxes, and other costs. Once these are paid, in theory, the notary reads the text of the Public Deed of Sale and asks for the approval of the parties, and the parties then sign, followed by the notary's signature and seal. In practice, the parties usually go to the secretary of the notary, and read and sign the deed, which is then later signed and sealed by the notary. The notary keeps the original deed in his or her records for 30 years, after which it is sent to the public archives. The notary issues four authenticated copies, one each for the buyer, seller, and lender, and one for registration in the Registry of Public Documents.

5. *Registering the Deed*

The Public Deed of Sale, with petition and fee, is filed in the registration office covering that geographical area. The petition is recorded in a daily book of recordings with notations for the time and date of filing, an annual number, and the title, date, and place of the original document. A dated receipt for filing is issued. Transfer of the property relates back to this date, if the other aspects of registration are successful. Without filing, receipt, and recordation in the daily book, the transfer of title is void.

After filing, the deed is reviewed by the legal department of the office to ensure that it is adequate to transfer title, complies with legal requirements, and may be recorded. Upon approval, the legal department writes a qualification memorandum of the exact annotations that are to be recorded. The memorandum is then forwarded to the office of registration where the annotations are transcribed verbatim into the real property folio. The recording date, title of document, date of document, office of origin, and parties are entered as well. Evidence of recording that recites the date of recording, the number of its filing, and other details is forwarded to the interested parties.

B. A SAMPLE COLOMBIAN AGREEMENT OF SALE

Agreement for Sale of Real Property

Place and Date of Execution: Santafé de Bogotá, June 1, 2006.

Seller and Identification: Andrés Bello, C.C. [national identity number] _____

Buyer and Identification: Justo Arosemena, C.C. _____

1. *Object.* The Seller will sell to the Buyer and the latter will buy from the former, the property that is described below:

The property as object of this promise is located in the city of ____ with principal door of access with number ___, boundaries of which are determined in Clause Ten.

2. *Conveyance.* The promised property for sale was acquired by the Seller by purchase from Juan Fulano, by means of Public Deed

Number 162, of the 3rd day of May of 1997, issued by the Second Notary of the Notarial Group of Santafé de Bogotá, recorded in the real property registry, title number 0401262, of the Registry of Public Documents of Santafé de Bogotá.

3. *Other obligations.* The Seller shall convey ownership of the property, object of this agreement, free from mortgages, civil lawsuits, attachments, and in general free from any encumbrance or limitation to ownership rights and will be obliged to cure such title defects in such events as required by law.

4. *Price.* The price for the promised property for sale is Three Million pesos ($3.000.000), an amount that the Buyer will pay to the Seller as follows: at the time of signing this agreement Five Hundred Thousand pesos ($500.000) and the remaining amount of Two Million Five Hundred Thousand pesos ($2.500.000) at the time of execution of the Public Deed of Sale.

5. *Earnest money.* The amount of Five Hundred Thousand pesos ($500.000), that the Seller represents has been received from the Buyer, has been delivered as earnest money and will be considered a part of the purchase price at the time of compliance with the formal requirements of this agreement.

6. *Execution.* The Public Deed of Sale that will satisfy the requirement of this promised sale will be executed in the Second Notary of the Notarial Group of Santafé de Bogotá on the 28th day of June of 2006 at 3:00 p.m.

7. *Amendment.* Any amendments to the terms of this agreement shall be made in writing and shall be signed by both parties.

8. *Delivery.* On the date of execution of the Public Deed of Sale, the Seller will deliver the property to the Buyer with any improvements, annexes, uses, and easements.

9. *Expenses.* Any expenses arising out of the execution of this agreement, as well as those that are required for the execution of the Public Deed of Sale and taxes shall be borne equally by the Seller and Buyer.

10. *Boundaries.* The boundaries of the property that is the object of this agreement are as follows:

Additional Terms:

As evidence of the above, the parties sign two originals for the parties on the 1st day of June of 2006.

Seller and C.C.   Buyer and C.C.

Witness and C.C.   Witness and C.C.

C. TITLE DEFECTS IN COLOMBIA

In the United States, the buyer secures protection against title defects by negotiating deed warranties, buying title insurance, or taking other voluntary actions. In Colombia, the buyer receives title protection by statute.

Civil Code of Colombia

Art. 1914. The buyer has an action of rescission (redhibitoria) to rescind the sale or to reduce proportionally the price for hidden defects in the thing sold, real or movable. . . .

Art. 1915. Such defects have the following characteristics:

1. existed at the time of sale;

2. are of such nature that the thing sold will not serve or will improperly serve its natural purpose in such a way that if those defects were known to the buyer, the buyer would not have purchased or would have purchased at a much lesser price;

3. the seller did not disclose them and are such that the buyer, because of the buyer's profession or occupation, would not have been able to notice them easily.

Art. 1916. If it were stipulated that the seller was not obligated to cure hidden defects in the thing, the seller is nevertheless obligated to cure those known by the seller and not disclosed to the buyer.

Notes

1. What are the most important differences between the typical residential sale transaction in the United States and in Colombia?

2. Can these differences be understood as reflecting different legal cultures? Does the greater reliance placed on registration in Colombia account for all these differences? Registration of title is discussed in more detail in Chapter 12.

3. How are title defects handled in the sales transaction in the United States, as compared to Colombia? What about physical defects in the property? Why do Colombians consider it unnecessary to deal with these in greater specificity in the agreement?

4. How do the title protections arising under the Colombian Civil Code compare to those provided by a general warranty deed in the United States?

5.   Chapter 13 describes the movement toward a uniform, international system of electronic land sales transactions. How might the differences revealed by Colombian practices, as an example, inform the creation of such a global system?

Chapter 12

TITLE ASSURANCE

A. INTRODUCTION TO TITLE REGISTRATION

A system of land registration helps to facilitate the efficient and safe transfer of real property. By developing a system that is both public and secure, land titles can be more effectively transferred and maintained.

Systems of land registration developed as societies became more complex and interrelated. Within small, geographically-isolated communities, visible, symbolic acts were effective means of acknowledging one's ownership interests. In medieval England and tribal Germany, for example, land was transferred by ritualistic handing-over of possession (livery of seisin and *Gewere*, respectively). These acts produced a degree of publicity that fostered the stabilization of ownership rights within the community. However, as communities became larger and more complex, and interaction between the community and strangers more frequent, these symbolic acts lost much of their value. New systems for ensuring the security of land titles were needed. Systems based on the public recording of real property interests accordingly emerged.

Throughout the world, there are numerous types of title protection systems. They differ in methodology, content, organization, and prominence. Generally, most seek to create a system of public records for the recognition and protection of land titles. This public visibility makes the process of transferring interests in land simpler and more efficient. The role of recordation or registration in the title assurance process varies from jurisdiction to jurisdiction. In particular, the common law and civil law traditions produced unique systems.

105

Alejandro M. Garro
Recordation of Interests in Land

Chapter 8, International Encyclopedia of Comparative Law 52–54 (2004)

French-Inspired Legal Systems.—The basic tenet of the FRENCH legal system and those following its model is that ownership (be it of movable or immovable property) is transferred by consent alone, without the need of further formalities. . . .

Recordation in FRENCH law, however, is not required to perfect or complete a conveyance but merely to set up or oppose the transfer *vis-à-vis* those who did not take part in the transaction (the so-called third persons or *tiers*), which includes not only subsequent purchasers or transferees but also creditors of the seller or transferor. In a large group of CIVIL LAW jurisdictions that includes SPAIN, PORTUGAL, ITALY, and most of LATIN AMER-ICA recordation is also vested with mere declarative effects, in the sense that it declares the existence of a right previously created by a legal transaction. The declarative effect of the act of recordation is thus expressed in SPANISH CC art. 606: "Title to ownership and other real rights less than ownership are of no effect as against third parties unless they have properly been entered into the land records."

Recordation in FRENCH law and FRENCH-inspired legal systems is therefore characterized by the central role played by the consent of the parties in the process of land transfer. This consent may be embodied first in a pre-contract (*avant-contrat*) or prelimi-nary agreement to sell and to buy (*compromis*) that later ripens into a veritable contract of sale. . . . A corollary of the declaratory nature of the act of recordation is that the mere fact that an instrument has become part of the public records by virtue of the act of recordation does not guarantee the truthfulness of its recitals nor the validity of the transaction. In other words: recordation makes the transaction effective against third persons but it does not give a creditor greater rights against third persons than he has against the person whose property is encumbered.

In most FRENCH-inspired legal systems the sales contract, as well as any other legal transactions subject to recordation, must be embodied in a notarial (authentic) act or, if submitted in a private writing, the signatures of the parties may be required to be certi-fied by a notary public. The contribution of the notary public to the smooth running of the recording office is worth noticing. Being a legally trained quasi-public official, the CIVIL LAW notary is bound to examine the entries in the land records, to inform the parties, in the instrument of transfer that he drafts, of entries of encum-brances, and to apply for recordation. . . .

Germanic-Inspired Legal Systems.—[I]n GERMAN law and in GERMANIC-inspired legal systems (e.g. AUSTRIA, SWITZER-LAND), the consensual transfer of any interest or right *in rem* affecting immovable property is carried out by a contract (*Einigung*) embodied in a notarial act. It is also a feature of the land conveyancing process in these countries that the parties must draw up their sales contract in a notarial instrument (*Grundstückskaufvertrag*). However, in GERMAN law, the conveyance or actual transfer does not take effect unless a formal declaration of conveyance made in the presence of a notary public (*Auflassung*) is entered into the land records (*Eintragung*). Accordingly, GERMAN CC § 873 provides that the transfer, acquisition, alteration or loss of any right *in rem* requires not only an agreement to that effect (*Einigung*), but also the recordation (*Eintragung*) in the land records. Since recordation is an essential requirement of the transfer of ownership and the creation or transfer of any other right *in rem*, it has constitutive effects. This feature is shared by several CIVIL LAW countries influenced by the GERMAN Civil Code, though details may vary. . . .

Thus, unlike FRENCH law, GERMAN law distinguished between an "obligatory agreement" represented by the contract of sale and the "real agreement". . . . It is possible, and in fact quite usual, for both agreements to be contained in a single document, especially when the same notary public handles both acts and keeps them in his protocol. . . . Ownership in GERMAN law is therefore acquired only after recordation (*Eintragung*) in the proper land records (*Grundbuch*). The notary public is in charge of filing a request for recordation at the recording office (*Grundbuchamt*). The notary describes the property to be purchased or encumbered on the basis of his or her inspection of the land records, lists all existing encumbrances in the purchase agreement, and informs the parties of these entries. It is worth repeating that the experienced advice of a notary public, who is bound to ensure that the interests of both the purchaser and the seller are taken into account, plays a significant role in the land transfer process. Potential sources of litigation, such as the parties' lack of consensus, misdescriptions of the property *etc.* are considerably reduced due to the compulsory intervention of the notary public.

Notes

1.   In the United States, a deed need not be recorded to effect a binding transfer of title. A conveyance is legally operative and valid between the parties if both (a) the Statute of Frauds is satisfied and (b) the deed is delivered. However, recordation is important to protect the grantee from the claims of third parties. Is this approach closer to the French model or the German model?

2. What are the costs and benefits of the German system, in which rights in land are only transferred through recordation? How do these compare to the costs and benefits of the Torrens system of title registration, which is used in Hawaii and a number of other states?

3. In both the French and German systems, the notary public has a much greater role in land transactions than in the United States. The notary is a quasi-public figure who actively examines the instruments of transfer and inspects the land records. Should the United States require greater training of, and more responsibilities for, its notaries? Does our system's greater reliance on real estate attorneys, title abstractors, and title insurance companies produce a less efficient system?

4. Think about how you would organize a system of title registration. Other than computerizing all records, are there additional approaches that can enhance the system's effectiveness? In Germany, each district keeps a folio for every parcel of land. Each folio contains sections of differing colored papers. The first section consists of white papers and identifies the property. The second section is pink and lists the names of the parties in interest and how the property was acquired. The third section of yellow papers contains cross-references to other interests (such as servitudes) that may exist in the parcel. The final green section lists security interests (such as mortgages) and indicates whether they have been extinguished or assigned. Can the simple process of using different colored papers help maximize the system's utility and minimize recording errors?

B. TITLE REGISTRATION AND MARKET STIMULATION

Development of an effective land registration system can have great economic and social significance. The creation of a dependable public record fosters economic growth by creating confidence in titles, thereby allowing real property to serve as a basis of credit. Studies in the Philippines established that a working registration system can raise the value of property by more than one-third; and research in Indonesia demonstrated that an inefficient system of recordation can add between 10% and 30% to the cost of a real estate transaction. Other studies reveal that over half of the loans to new businesses in the United States depend principally on the strength of land titles—strength that is in large part created by our system of recordation.

Hernando de Soto
The Mystery of Capital

5–7 (2001)

[B]lock by block and farm by farm in Asia, Africa, the Middle East, and Latin America...most of the poor already possess the assets they need to make a success of capitalism. Even in the poorest countries, the poor save. . . .

But they hold these resources in defective forms: houses built on land whose ownership rights are not adequately recorded, unincorporated businesses with undefined liability, industries located where financiers and investors cannot see them. Because the rights to these possessions are not adequately documented, these assets cannot readily be turned into capital, cannot be traded outside of narrow local circles where people know and trust each other, cannot be used as collateral for a loan, and cannot be used as a share against an investment.

In the West, by contrast, every parcel of land, every building, every piece of equipment, or store of inventories is represented in a property document that is the visible sign of a vast hidden process that connects all these assets to the rest of the economy. Thanks to this representational process, assets can lead an invisible, parallel life alongside their material existence. They can be used as collateral for credit. The single most important source of funds for new businesses in the United States is a mortgage on the entrepreneur's house. These assets can also provide a link to the owner's credit history, an accountable address for the collection of debts and taxes, the basis for the creation of reliable and universal public utilities, and a foundation for the creation of securities (like mortgage-backed bonds) that can then be rediscounted and sold in the secondary markets. By this process the West injects life into assets and makes them generate capital.

Third World and former communist nations do not have this representational process. As a result, most of them are undercapitalized, in the same way that a firm is undercapitalized when it issues fewer securities than its income and assets would justify. The enterprises of the poor are very much like corporations that cannot issue shares or bonds to obtain new investment and finance. Without representations, their assets are dead capital.

The poor inhabitants of these nations—five-sixths of humanity—do have things, but they lack the process to represent their property and create capital. They have houses but not titles; crops but not deeds; businesses but not statutes of incorporation. It is the unavailability of these essential representations that explains why people who have adapted every other Western invention, from the paper clip to the nuclear reactor, have not been able to produce sufficient capital to make their domestic capitalism work. . . .

Notes

1. De Soto posits that a formal system for titling, recording, and mapping real property is essential for the economic progress of develop-

ing countries. Is the connection between (a) a land market supported by public records and (b) the production of economic well-being as robust as de Soto indicates? Why?

2. As an example of the barriers that face the poor within their world of ill-defined property rights, de Soto points to his team's attempt to obtain legal authorization to build a house on state-owned land in Peru—it took almost seven years to perform the necessary 207 administrative steps at the more than 52 governmental offices. An integrated system of public registration, he argues, would produce more clearly defined and enforceable property rights, leading to a larger information base and greater access to credit.

3. De Soto is not without critics. Many argue that Western systems and notions of capitalism are ill-suited for other regions. Differing histories, values, and customs create societies with different political and legal systems. Some may be more "culturally friendly" to formalized systems of recordation; others may be socially and economically disadvantaged by Western approaches to land registration. The material that follows makes this point.

C. TITLE REGISTRATION AND CUSTOMARY LAW

A number of developing countries are redesigning and modernizing their land title systems. Under the direction of the World Bank, many have adopted Western versions of land registration. However, the transition to a formalized recording system is often difficult. Capturing long-held customary rights within a formal system of registration can cause significant complications, including the reorganization, transformation, and, sometimes, destruction of the property rights of the poorer and less powerful members of society.

Daniel Fitzpatrick

Disputes and Pluralism in Modern Indonesian Land Law

22 Yale J. Int'l L. 171, 172–73, 180–82, 188–89, 205–06 (1997)

The Preamble to Indonesia's Basic Agrarian Law of 1960 ("the BAL") states that the current land law of Indonesia is incompatible with the interests of the people and the state, as it is based upon the objectives and principles of the colonial government. The Explanatory Memorandum expands on this notion by explaining that the pluralism of colonial land law, in which diverse customary (adat) laws existed alongside Western-style statutory law, is inconsistent with nation-building and fails to provide legal certainty to...Indonesians. The BAL's stated objective, therefore, is to lay the foundation for a national agrarian law that provides legal unity, simplicity, and certainty to all Indonesians, and prosperity, happiness, and justice for the nation and the people, including farming communities. The BAL seeks to do this in the syncretic way beloved by Indonesians: on the one hand, it converts all existing statutory rights, and most adat rights, into a range of Western–style, registrable land rights; on the other hand, it explains that these rights are based upon adat law and have a social function that emphasizes the needs of the community over those of the individual.

Thirty-six years later, it is apparent that the BAL's objectives of legal unity and certainty have not been attained and will not be attained in the foreseeable future. The Indonesian government estimates that no more than twenty percent of all registrable land, and only ten percent in rural areas, has been registered under the BAL. The number and severity of disputes over land have increased dramatically. Large tracts of newly settled areas, both urban and rural, now exist without the certainties that established adat authority or the BAL can provide....

[The BAL] operates contrary to adat, particularly in its imposition of Western-style, individualized land titles on customary forms of tenure. This inconsistency with adat has two fundamental consequences. First, the process of registering titles under the BAL itself creates long-term disputation and social conflict, and, for that reason, is highly unlikely to fulfill its objective of legal certainty. Second, the BAL's failure to provide legal certainty, in combination with the erosion or subjugation of adat authority in many areas, has created a dangerous legal vacuum and allowed ad hoc bureaucratic fiat to dominate the administration and development of land in Indonesia....

The Nature of Adat Land Law

[A]dat land law recognizes a number of individual rights to land, including rights to possess, use, harvest, pledge, lease, and priority to buy. The nature and strength of these rights vary from region to region. They are most common in urban areas and in Java, but far less prevalent in West Sumatra, Bali, Kalimantan, and Irian Jaya. Their strength also depends on where the land to which they relate is situated. Individual rights are less likely to be subject to communal control when they exist in agricultural fields not subject to wet rice-farming. Communal controls are more likely to exist in situations involving wet rice-farming, village housing, and religious land.

Traditionally, these community controls over individual rights are said to be embodied in the overarching community right of disposal known by Dutch scholars as bescchikkingsrecht and by Indonesian lawyers as hak ulayat. Hak ulayat has two basic features. The first is the way in which the relationship between an individual community member's right to land and the community's right of disposal turns on an ebb and flow of commitment and obligation. That is to say, the more work and capital that an individual puts into a piece of land, the greater the community's recognition of the individual's particular right to it; the less work put into a piece of land by an individual, the more likely that the community will exercise its overarching right to reallocate the land for another member's use.

The second feature is that the transfer of rights, whether to outsiders or between individual community members, is subject to strict community control. At most, outsiders can obtain limited rights of use to land only with the consent of the community and on the payment of "recognition money" (recognitie). Similarly, community members generally can only acquire rights to land from other community members with the consent of the community or its heads. . . .

[I]ndividual rights to use or possess adat lands are also commonly subject to obligations to provide voluntary labor to the community, communal rights of free passage and grazing in non-crop seasons, communal rights to excise land or redivide fields to accommodate an increased population, communal restrictions on changes of use, and neighbors' rights of first options to purchase in the event of alienation. In some areas, maintenance of adat rights to land is also tied to performance of fundamental ritual and ceremonial obligations.

The Incompatibility of Adat and the BAL

The Western nature of the BAL's rights, the unregistrability of hak ulayat, and the inability to register other communal rights all suggest that the BAL, at least as currently applied, is ultimately directed at the individualization of land tenure in Indonesia. Many view such an imposition of Western-style tenure as a precondition for economic development. . . . But it is clear that adat land law is cognizable only in the context of communal rights and obligations, which are underpinned by social processes of consensus, discussion, and deliberation. Individualizing and "freezing" tenure through a process of registering Western-style rights threatens to break down this subtle interaction between individuals and their community. In doing so, individual registration of land also threatens traditional village social structure itself, at least to the extent that this structure is based on communal and cooperative elements. As a result, rather than conferring legal unity and certainty, the registration of rights under the BAL is far more likely to lead to disputation, de facto pluralism, and ultimately the erosion of adat authority itself. This erosion will only accelerate as land acquires increased economic value under the pressures of industrialization, urbanization, and population growth. . . .

In other words, where the land law on which title registrations are based is inconsistent with social reality, the much-touted benefit of registration—increased certainty that leads to increased investment and access to formal credit—does not materialize. Instead, registration engenders conflict and bifurcates local practice and state law. In turn, this bifurcation generates a vicious developmental cycle in which economic activity is neither instigated by local communities nor negotiated through them. Instead, it is imposed from above in an ad hoc and discriminatory way by an alliance of bureaucracy and private commercial interests. . . .

Solely committing further resources to the process of title registration, without reforming the BAL and associated areas, will not resolve the problems with modern Indonesian land law and administration. The problems require a holistic solution that addresses issues of dispute resolution, access to credit, compulsory acquisition, corruption, unlawful occupancy, and, above all, the relationship between adat and the state.

Notes

1. The Indonesian adat is loosely defined as a tribe, family, or other group of individuals whose land belongs communally to the members of the group. Because adat law is so embedded in local social structure and so lacking in Western legal predictability, it is hard to incorporate its principles of title into a country-wide, formal system of registration. Fitzpatrick urges that a range of registration choices be made available to more fairly reflect the regional diversity of adats in Indonesia. Can such a mixed system be effective? How would disputes about title between adats be handled? Fitzpatrick suggests creating a separate, national Land Court to deal with dispute resolution.

2. Why isn't the development of a formalized land registration system simply a matter of technical mapping and recording?

3. Joel Ngugi has contended that adopting Western registration systems has not necessarily led to more land security or a better basis for developing needed collateral. Analyzing the Kenyan experience, Ngugi found that the registration system channeled land into the hands of certain elite groups, rather than preserving the entitlements that had existed under customary rules and practices. He noted that the registration system often reshaped community values and created destabilizing factors in Kenyan society. *See* Joel M. Ngugi, *Re-Examining the Role of Private Property in Market Democracies: Problematic Ideological Issues Raised by Land Registration*, 25 Mich. J. Int'l L. 467 (2004).

4. In some developing countries, government officials and their representatives are viewed as corrupt, dishonest, or incompetent. If individuals do not trust officials to properly record and maintain land titles, can a formal registration system be effective? How can this problem be successfully addressed?

5. For additional approaches to title assurance, see Joyce Palomar, *Land Tenure Security as a Market Stimulator in China*, 12 Duke J. Comp. & Int'l L. 7 (2002) and Philip von Mehren & Tim Sawers, *Revitalizing the Law and Development Movement: A Case Study of Title in Thailand*, 33 Harv. Int'l L.J. 67 (1992).

Chapter 13

LAND SALES AND INTERNATIONAL LAW

Land sales transactions increasingly reach across national borders. Citizens of Great Britain buy vacation homes in France; German companies purchase shopping centers in the United States; and multinational corporations buy hotels around the world.

Currently, these transactions are governed by national law—and often by local law. Will an international land sale system eventually emerge? Experts suggest that the evolution of a global system may be inevitable, given present trends. At a minimum, existing national and local property law systems may evolve toward more global uniformity in some respects. What standards might govern international land sales transactions?

A. LAND SALES IN THE UNITED STATES: A LOCAL MATTER

An overview of the land sale system in the United States provides a useful foundation for the balance of this chapter. Traditionally, we have viewed the land sales transaction as a local matter, governed by state law. But national developments have increasingly affected these transactions in recent decades. The number of interstate sales transactions has risen dramatically, fueled by consumer demand for vacation homes in other states, the growth of companies that invest in real estate in multiple states, and other factors. Thus, today it is not unusual for a resident of State A to purchase land in State B. Moreover, the infrastructure that facilitates land sales has become more national in scope. Listings of property available for sale can now be accessed on the internet. The lending and title insurance industries operate on a national scale, which has produced more uniformity; thus, loan documents and title insurance policies tend to be somewhat standardized across the country. Finally, federal law now has a role—if a minor one—in regulating some land sales. Thus, there is a slow trend toward a national approach.

Yet we do not have a national land market in the United States in the same way that we have, for example, a national stock market. A person in any state can purchase stock quickly and easily by an e-mail or phone call to a broker. Land sales, however, are still predominantly local in character. Why? The reasons include: (1) land description and mapping techniques are not standardized (e.g., we still use metes and bounds descriptions); (2) public land records are maintained on a local basis; (3) the sales process is still based on paper documents, which must be physically signed and transported; (4) most sales listings are still local in scope; and (5) the laws governing property rights and contracts vary from state to state.

B. LAND SALES IN ENGLAND AND WALES: MODEL FOR A GLOBAL SYSTEM

A national land sale system is now emerging in England and Wales, which may serve as a model for a global system. The centerpiece of this system is the electronic sales transaction, which necessitates a paperless, standardized land sale system, administered on a national basis under national statutes by Her Majesty's Land Registry. Under this system: (1) electronic sales contracts will replace paper contracts; (2) land description and surveying techniques are standardized; (3) title to almost all land in England and Wales is now "registered" with the national Land Registry and title information is stored electronically; (4) buyers and their attorneys can easily search title to almost any parcel by accessing the Land Registry records via the internet; (5) escrows will be handled electronically by the Land Registry, which will manage the exchange of all funds, including the buyer's deposit, loan funds, and all tax payments; and (6) new titles will be registered electronically.

Thus, a resident of England will be able to purchase title to a tract of land in Wales almost as easily as she might purchase a share of stock, once the system is operational. Of course, the system is designed to accommodate relatively simple, routine transactions, such as the sale of a single-family home or a vacant lot. More complex transactions will be handled within the system, to the extent possible, but will inevitably need some individualized treatment.

Land Registry, United Kingdom
The Strategy for the Implementation of
E–Conveyancing in England and Wales

8, 12, 16, 18–19 (2005)

...As countries throughout the world feel the impact and benefit of electronic commerce, there is a general feeling that conveyancing must move with the times, and governments, particularly in Europe, Canada and Australaisa, are investigating proposals for electronic systems of land transfer.

Ideas for re-engineering the conveyancing process in England and Wales have been developing over a number of years. In 1998, preliminary proposals were set out in the joint report by the Law Commission and Land Registry entitled "*Land Registration for the Twenty–First Century*"... Since then, a series of consultations with stakeholders by government has enabled further development of these ideas. ...

At the same time, the business environment generally has been experiencing a steady move towards electronic commerce. Citizens expect to be able to deal on-line with government and business; they also expect services to be faster and more reliable, and businesses and government services are responding to this demand. Lenders, conveyancers and estate agents are all developing on-line services that exploit the opportunities of the new technologies. ...

Land Registry currently operates one of the largest databases of property information in the world. Over 20 million registered titles within England and Wales are held electronically and updated by Land Registry staff. Land Registry Direct allows a range of services to be carried out from PCs in practitioners' own offices over the internet. In March 2003, Land Registry introduced Land Register Online, its first internet based online service for the general public to access information from the Land Register. ...

[Our vision is] a world class conveyancing service, where:

- the worry and risk of the conveyancing process are significantly reduced;

- authorised parties involved in a conveyancing transaction can exchange information quickly, securely and reliably with each other and with Land Registry;

- registration will be confirmed immediately on completion;

- up-to-date and accurate information is available on the progress of all linked conveyancing transactions; and

- funds can be transferred immediately, securely and reliably.

    . . .

While some details of the infrastructure that will underpin the vision remain to be finalised, the re-engineered process is expected to incorporate the following new features:

- At the time the seller's conveyancer uses the E–Conveyancing service to transmit the draft contract from his case management system to the buyer's conveyancer, automatic validation checks would compare contract data with Land Registry data and electronic messages would indicate any discrepancies. . . .

- Conveyancers would also record on the system the stage reached on each transaction. This would enable the conveyancers and Land Registry to see the progress of all the transactions linked together in a chain. . . .

- At the contract stage, there would be an electronic equivalent of the present exchange of contracts. Contracts would be exchanged electronically when buyer's and seller's conveyancers had signaled that agreement had been reached and contracts had been signed and released for electronic exchange. . . . For this and other purposes, conveyancers will need to have electronic signatures and authentication from a recognised Certification Authority. . . .

- A substantive register entry would be made to note the contract; the Register would automatically be frozen and would provide a priority period for the ensuing registration on completion [close of escrow]. . . .

- During this period the draft electronic transfer and any draft electronic charges will be agreed and finalised. These documents will then be signed electronically in anticipation of completion just as they are in the existing paper system. . . .

- Registration [of title] would take place with completion. . . .

- All financial obligations, including Stamp Duty Land Tax and Land Registry fees as well as payments between buyers, sellers, lenders and conveyancers, would be settled through an Electronic Funds Transfer system. . . .

Notes

1. The Land Registry plans to introduce e-conveyancing in increments, and the complete system may not be in place until after 2010. The plan is that use of e-conveyancing will be voluntary, so paper-based transactions will continue. However, many observers predict that e-conveyancing will become compulsory at some future point. E-conveyancing is already in place, on a smaller scale, in New Zealand and in part of Canada.

2. Great Britain is the world's fourth-largest property market, measured by land value. One commentator notes that Britain has been at the cutting edge of world commerce for centuries and "has consciously developed its laws to accommodate inward investment and invisible exports—the same applies to e-conveyancing." Carolyn Owen, *Is E–Conveyancing Coming Home?*, 152 New L.J. 7060 (2002). She stresses the "need to accommodate the global market as well as the domestic: we will creating a winning system of e-conveyancing." *Id.* Should the English approach be adopted as the global standard?

C. INTERNATIONAL LAND SALES: TOWARD A GLOBAL SYSTEM

What would a global land sale system look like? Perhaps it might include some of the following components:

Uniform property rights: The rights of landowners vary substantially from nation to nation. A global system might well require a more uniform definition of property rights, at least a minimum "package" of property rights that all nations would guarantee. For example, the package might include (1) the right to free alienation of property and (2) the right to receive the fair market value of the property upon any expropriation (see Chapter 16). The law of many countries, including the United States, recognizes these key rights.

Uniform land identification system: Each parcel of land must be uniquely identifiable through a standardized system, which is linked to an accurate survey, available via the internet. The e-conveyancing system in England and Wales includes this component, but the system in United States lags far behind. *See generally* Paul E. Bayse, *A Uniform Land Parcel Identifier—Its Potential for All Our Land Records*, 22 Am. U.L. Rev. 251 (1973).

Uniform land registration system: Experts agree that land title registration (discussed in Chapter 12) is the best system of title assurance in terms of cost, simplicity, and effectiveness. The land recordation system used in the United States, in contrast, is expensive, complex, and unreliable—and thus unlikely to be adopted as a global standard. *See generally* Tim Hanstad, *Designing Land Registration Systems for Developing Countries*, 13 Am. U. Int'l L. Rev. 647, 670–76 (1998). Note that registration is used in England and Wales.

Uniform contract law principles: A global system would require an enforceable body of international contract law applicable to land sales. The United Nations Convention on Contracts for the International Sale of Goods (1980) may be helpful here by analogy, as would the 2004 Unidroit Principles of International Commercial Contracts.

Electronic transaction system: Electronic transactions would be a key part of the global system. Contracts would be negotiated, land title would be checked, loan financing would be provided, and the transaction would be consummated—all electronically. As discussed above, the system in England and Wales will be almost wholly electronic. In contrast, electronic sales transactions are in their infancy in the United States. The Uniform Electronic Transactions Act and the federal Electronic Signatures in Global and National Commerce Act both permit electronic conveyances. However, they do not compel local recorder's offices to record electronic documents; thus, only a handful of recorder's offices permit electronic recording. The international community is moving toward standards for electronic commerce in general. For example, the United Nations Commission on International Trade Law (1) adopted a Model Law on Electronic Commerce in 1996 and (2) proposed a "United Nations Convention on the Use of Electronic Communications in International Contracts" in 2005; but neither appears to cover land sales transactions.

Notes

1. How likely is it that the current land sale system in the United States will become the future global system?

2. What impact would a global system have on property law in the United States?

Chapter 14

LAND USE REGULATION

A. LAND USE REGULATION IN CONTEXT

Public regulation of land use has been common throughout history. For example, Roman law provided for building restrictions and set-back lines as early as the fourth century B.C. Thus, even in the past, when vacant land was more plentiful and the population less dense than today, societies placed restrictions on the use of their physical space.

The United States has a long history of public control of land use. Modern land use regulation in our nation began in 1916 with the adoption of the first comprehensive zoning ordinance in New York City. A system of local zoning ordinances—which essentially separated uses into different zones, and regulated the height, bulk, and location of structures—became the distinctively American approach to land use regulation. With the widespread adoption of the Standard State Zoning Enabling Act in the 1920s, cities and counties across the nation adopted zoning ordinances based on this model. Even though the particular land use laws of municipalities may differ, most still share this common foundation. Land use regulation is predominantly viewed as a local matter; in general, states and the federal government have little or no role in this process.

Today we face increasingly complex land use problems. Urbanization, industrialization, environmental contamination, and other developments may threaten the public health, safety, and welfare. An exploration of land use regulation in other areas of the world quickly reveals a vast quilt of differing approaches. It is important to understand the alternatives that exist to our land use system, because they may help us meet the emerging needs of the twenty-first century.

B. LAND USE IN THE UNITED STATES, GERMANY, AND SWITZERLAND

The following excerpt compares the land use regimes of the United States, Germany, and Switzerland.

Matthew A. Light
Different Ideas of the City: Origins of Metropolitan Land–Use Regimes in the United States, Germany, and Switzerland

24 Yale J. Int'l L. 577, 577–78, 580–81, 584–592, 610–611 (1999)

[N]ational regimes of land-use regulation—the whole body of a country's institutions, laws, and jurisprudence that regulates building and development—can be understood only in the context of distinct political and legal regimes. National land-use regimes do not arise in response to universal laws of the market that exert the same influence at any location on the planet. Rather, land-use regimes differ from country to country. They are embedded in a complex, historically developing framework of ideology, law, and culture. If land-use controls regulate the physical shape of the communities we live in, then it is history itself that regulates what kind of community we view as wholesome, normal, and desirable— our ideas of what "the city" and "the good city" mean.

Much thinking about land-use topics in the United States seems to be predicated on the unspoken assumption that metropolitan development can only follow the pattern it has taken in the United States since World War II, namely that of business and residential expansion on the urban periphery, "dispersed in a pattern that can only be served by the single occupant auto." In fact, however, other countries have selected, and continue to pursue, radically different land-use regimes. By examining such alternatives to American policies, we are forced to confront the fact that much of what we take for granted about the American metropolitan scene can be traced to concrete political choices. Ultimately, the comparative approach helps demonstrate that Americans, like other peoples, have a particular idea of the good city; that our idea arises out of our history, culture, and legal doctrine; and that this idea can be recognized in many aspects of a country's regime of land-use regulation.

What follows is a comparative study of the land-use regimes of the United States, Germany, and Switzerland. . . . One may well question the differences between American and German–Swiss urban forms. Why do American cities sometimes merge with each other along lines of roads and highways, while Swiss towns are separated from each other by expanses of fields or woodland? Why do even affluent Germans tolerate small, expensive living quarters, while American suburbanites spread out in ever larger houses and lots? And why have German and Swiss cities largely succeeded in preserving a monopoly over retail establishments, even as American downtowns have emptied out in the face of competition from out-of-town shopping centers?

The short answer to these questions is that the legal regime governing land use in the United States does not share certain common features of the analogous regimes in the two European countries. The German and Swiss land-use regimes concentrate on the goal of preserving traditional, compact urban areas defined by legally established growth perimeters and ringed by countryside untouched by urbanization. American land-use controls, by contrast, do not attempt to preserve this traditional urban form, which has been eroding in the United States with particular rapidity since the beginning of the post-World War II economic boom....

[W]hile American land-use policies aim at the safeguarding of private life, German and Swiss policies aim at the shaping of public space. American policies feature fragmented decision-making, concentrated in municipalities, and focus on the protection of single-family residences. German and Swiss laws, by contrast, involve all levels of government in concert and are devoted to preserving a certain urban form: the compact city.

American land-use controls are marked by a few particularly noteworthy characteristics: the comparative weakness of overt involvement by state and federal government in local land-use controls; the corresponding delegation of land-use regulatory power to municipalities; the reliance on zoning as the preeminent method of local land-use controls and the relatively weak links between zoning and comprehensive land-use planning; and the ubiquitous use of zoning to effect the separation of "incompatible" residential and non-residential uses—and particularly the protection of single-family homes from "lower" uses.

One of the most noteworthy facts about land-use controls in the United States is the extreme localization (and consequently, fragmentation) of their implementation. Apart from some relatively recent environmental legislation, ... the federal government plays a fairly limited overt role in the land-use controls governing privately owned land....

[A] key feature of the American regime that distinguishes it from its German and Swiss counterparts—and that justifies a national-level comparison—is America's reliance on municipal zoning as the preeminent tool of metropolitan land-use regulation. Western European observers are frequently perplexed by the fact that zoning appears to exist in the absence of highly developed national (or even state) policies on land-use *planning*. . . .

American land-use law's reliance on zoning and the weakness of statutory urban planning can be understood relatively easily by reference to goals made explicit within zoning jurisprudence itself. Zoning in the United States has focused on one central objective: the separation of residential uses from others, and, within the broader category of residential uses, the separation of single-family homes from other kinds of living accommodations. Zoning accomplishes this goal admirably even without extensive city planning. As will be argued, American zoning law represents a rejection of urbanity and of the city in favor of a certain vision of private domestic life.

Zoning developed as a statutory tool intended to protect favored uses and households from disfavored ones. This phenomenon can be traced back as far as the foundational *Euclid* case, in which the Supreme Court gave its imprimatur to zoning by holding that the practice falls within the state's "police power." In its decision, the *Euclid* Court describes as the "crux" of zoning legislation "the creation and maintenance of residential districts, from which business and trade of every sort, *including hotels and apartment houses*, are excluded." To this day, American zoning is still based on a model of a "hierarchy" of uses, with single-family residences as the highest use, followed by multiple-family residences, commerce, light industry, and so forth. And "single-family dwellings were, and they continue to be, regarded as meriting the most stringent protection." . . .

Land-Use Regimes in Germany and Switzerland

German and Swiss land-use regimes diverge from the American model. . . . Fundamentally, they stem not from a glorification of private life, as in the United States, but rather from a subordination of private life and private property to a certain model of the normatively desirable community. The German and Swiss regimes give government full control over the location and extent of future development. And government employs this power so as to preserve the hegemony of important towns over their surrounding smaller towns, villages, and countryside.

In addition, the German and Swiss systems share a common structure involving all levels of administration: a federal government that frames the broad outlines of land-use policy and identifies the objectives of land-use controls; German states (*Länder;* singular, *Land*) and Swiss cantons that provide relatively detailed plans for the use of the territory under their jurisdiction; and, finally, regional and local administration of these plans, including zoning and direct control over individual land parcels. In both countries the basic system of land-use controls is laid out in a federal law.

The Land–Use Regime of Germany

Thus, in Germany, the federal *Bundesraumordnungsgesetz* (Federal Land–Use Law, hereinafter BROG) sets out the goals of land-use regulation and the means of their implementation in a general and nonhierarchical manner. The BROG requires each German *Land* to formulate a program and comprehensive plans for its own territory. This state-level planning (*Landesplanung*) is intended to produce a development program (*Landesentwicklungsprogramm*) with a lifespan of about fifteen years. This program divides the territory of the state into regions; for example, the relatively large German *Land* of Bavaria is divided into eighteen planning regions. Within each of these regions the government assigns a particular status to the various cities, towns, and villages within the state, based on their size and importance. . . .

[R]estrictions on development cannot be evaded by moving out of town altogether, as they can be in the United States. To begin, in contrast to the United States, nearly all German land lies within the territory of a municipality. This means that it is not possible, as it is in the United States, for a developer to evade the zoning plan of a municipality by relocating her building activities a mile or two beyond the city limit. More fundamentally, the use of nonurban (i.e., primarily agricultural) land, which has received the legal designation of *Aussenbereich*, or "outside area," is regulated with great strictness in Germany. Under German law, building on such land is essentially limited to construction ancillary to agricultural activities. In short, in Germany there is no escape from regional land-use regulation and national land-use policy.

Finally, in further contrast to the United States, the power of the federal government and *Länder* also extends to the control of land-use regulation enacted by local government. Under the German Federal Building Code, each municipality is required to draw up zoning plans (*Flächennutzungspläne*) and, at the most detailed level, building plans (*Bebauungspläne*), that regulate individual subdivisions. These plans are subject to higher-level review. For example, the *Land* of Schleswig–Holstein reviews "[local] development plans, which are drafted for a period of five years, and may disapprove the plans if they do not meet federal and state planning goals." Thus, Germany's land-use regime is both more hierarchical and more comprehensive than America's. Do Germans tolerate these restraints on the use of private property because they are more left-wing than Americans, as evidenced by Germany's strong labor unions and historically Marxist left? No. Rather, German land-use controls represent a consensus on what constitutes the model of the good urban life. This model is embraced not just by the concededly rather social democratic Germans, but by their decidedly free-market neighbors, the Swiss.

The Land–Use Regime of Switzerland

The Swiss Federation's power to implement a national land-use policy is derived from a constitutional amendment adopted only as recently as 1967. By this amendment the Swiss federal government was empowered to enact legislation to establish basic principles with respect to the development and settlement of the nation and the use of land, and in particular the creation of zoning regulations by the cantons. Under the constitution, the federation is also authorized to promote and coordinate the land-use regulation activities of the cantons. As can be readily observed, this range of powers corresponds closely to that exercised by the federal government of Germany.

On the strength of this new constitutional provision, the Swiss government later enacted land-use legislation, known as the *Bundesgesetz über die Raumplanung* (RPG) of 1979. Like the German BROG, the RPG establishes general rules to which all levels of government must adhere. In addition, the RPG allocates responsibilities among different levels of government. Thus, the federation's duties include consultation with the cantons, regular reporting on the current land-use situation, and (more substantially) the elaboration of certain *Sachpläne*, plans over specific policy areas.

As to the cantons, the RPG directs them to produce development programs (*Richtpläne*), similar to those of the German *Länder*, in which the cantons are to report on the current condition and development of population, traffic, and so forth. The cantons must specify the time framework for the implementation of their program, and the *Richtpläne* are also to be reexamined and, if necessary, reworked every ten years. The cantons must also designate which areas are most suitable for agriculture or are deserving of protection because of their beauty, cultural significance, or susceptibility to environmental problems. In addition, the cantons are directed to produce more specific use plans, or *Nutzungspläne*, which actually carve up their territory into several different use zones; these plans are normally drawn up by the communes (i.e., municipalities) on the orders of the cantonal governments. The main use zones are the building zones (*Bauzonen*), the agricultural zones (*Landwirtschaftszonen*), and the conservation zones (*Schutzzonen*).

Because it prohibits urbanization of agricultural zones, the RPG ensures that agricultural land is protected, while land available for development is contained and monopolized by existing centers. In addition, the RPG specifies that building zones can encompass only land that is already developed or whose necessary development is foreseeable within a span of fifteen years. Thus, it becomes clear that it is *new development* that the RPG views as the proper object of restraint and suspicion.

As for the cantons, they use their land-use powers in accordance with the same broad goals as those underlying the RPG. For example, the 1985 *Baugesetz* (Building and Planning Code) of the canton of Bern provides a useful illustration of the actual implementation of the national policy on the cantonal level.

Within the canton of Bern, planning and zoning responsibilities are meticulously divided and coordinated among different levels of government. Thus, the cantonal administration itself is responsible for the publication of reports on land use, for the delineation of agricultural land, for the establishment of cantonal development plans when the communes or the regions fail to safeguard interests broader than their own, and for the development plans required by the RPG.

Below the cantonal level, the regions and communes of the canton of Bern also play an important role in land-use regulation. These "regions" are groups of communes agglomerated for the purposes of land-use control. As Zaugg explains, "The region in the sense of land-use planning law is a space that is characterized and limited by geographic features...and by economic relationships and interdependence." The regions are responsible for land-use regulation tasks that require coordination among the member communes. They also serve as an intermediate level and liaison between the cantonal government and the communes.

Finally, at the most local level, the municipalities are bound by the federal constitution and legislation and by cantonal legislation. However, it is also the communes that actually zone their own territory and regulate subdivision development and actual buildings. In addition, they are responsible for supplying authorized developments with public utilities and roads and for the consolidation of building areas. Thus, the example of Bern demonstrates how Swiss and German land-use law integrates all governmental bodies into an effort to pursue a national policy....

The German and Swiss Regimes: Goals

The German and Swiss land-use laws share a number of objectives. Broadly speaking, the laws are formulated to prevent destabilizing social change. Swiss and German policies evince a refusal to treat land-use regulation in the American manner, as essentially a matter of regulating private property rights; in contrast, Swiss and German laws assume that land-use regulation is an important way of maintaining the social order.

This broad goal of maintaining social stability is instantiated in more specific policy objectives. These include the stabilization of small cities' populations by preventing large-scale migration for economic reasons; the prevention of sprawl and the preservation of the appearance of both cities and countryside; and the promotion of commercial agriculture and especially family farmers. Let us consider these concerns in turn, using examples drawn from both Germany and Switzerland.

First, by closing off the overwhelming mass of agricultural land to development through the legal categories of *Aussenbereich* in Germany and *Landwirtschaftszone* in Switzerland, existing cities in effect receive a monopoly of most nonagricultural economic activity, and population growth is directed to existing centers. The designation of towns as "centers" of different ranks, or as non-centers, also serves this goal. That is, by restricting development in minor centers and non-centers, German policy discourages people from moving to areas where, by definition, housing, jobs, and services will not be provided. Like the strict controls on building in the *Aussenbereich* and in the *Landwirtschaftszonen*, the policy of "center" designation thus appears to stem from a desire to limit internal migration and keep people where they already are....

Second, Swiss and German concern is not just with migration of persons between cities; it is also with migration of persons, and businesses, from towns into the hinterland. An important principle of the BROG requires the territory of Germany to be developed so as to construct "a balanced relationship between populated areas and rural space." Stripped of the pleasing rhetoric, this policy means that existing downtowns receive a monopoly of most economic functions in order to prevent development from spilling out into the countryside. Again, the goal can be described at its highest level of generality as preservation of the traditional compact city.

Swiss law also uses national policy to preserve urban cores. For example, Bernese law discourages the development of large shopping centers outside existing downtowns by requiring municipal authorization and supervision of any such projects. This prohibition is unapologetically intended, in part, *to protect such downtowns from competition*. The Bernese model of city development calls for "decentralization of settlement and economy," in other words, the preservation of numerous viable population centers. It is worth noting in this context that U.S. courts have frequently been confronted with the anti-competitive implications of comprehensive plans designed to protect downtown merchants. While such plans have generally withstood litigation, the fact that the issue is raised at all indicates how controversial and sometimes offensive down-town-protection can seem in an American legal context. . . .

Conclusion: Land–Use Regimes as Responses to Modernity

The differences between American and German–Swiss attitudes to land-use are so profound that they lie embedded and hidden in the foundations of public life, rather than visible in the political structures.

Thus, in post-World War II Germany and Switzerland, governments recognized the threat to the traditional urban form inherent in an affluent society characterized by a widespread desire for upward economic mobility that was expressed in the aspiration for home and car ownership. Officials resolved to manage economic growth to preserve the land-use status quo. In short, land-use regulation for the Swiss and the Germans is a way of restraining the modern economy to protect a traditional way of life. It enforces a prescriptive model of the good city and of the good countryside, and requires the market to operate within that model.

Indeed, German and Swiss views of land-use have evolved to the point where a national land-use regime is seen as an essential part of the construction of the polity. As one Swiss land-use expert has put it, land-use planning is part of the state's ongoing responsibility to guarantee "the preconditions of life" (*"Lebensvoraussetzungen"*). He writes of Switzerland's national land-use planning: "Its object—briefly summarized—is living space (*Lebensraum*), that is, the space in which life is to be preserved and in which individual and social life develops."

Contemporary America, on the other hand, is so remote from the German and Swiss idea of the town that there is no intellectual basis for duplicating land-use controls which derive from that idea. We cannot simply scrap the ideological background that gave us the metropolitan form we do have. The American public law hostility to the city has left a heavy ideological mortgage. . . .

If German and Swiss land-use regulations place the individual in the center of a managed landscape and a restrictive community, American land-use regulation seems to reject this idea of a socially situated self. If German and Swiss land-use policies reflect a dogged determination to control the modern town and make it conform to an inherited idea of the well-made community, American land-use controls represent a willingness to experiment with unprecedented forms of urban life.

Notes

1.   What are the strengths and weaknesses of the land use regime in the United States as compared to the German and Swiss systems?

2. What tradeoffs would be necessary if the United States adopted either the German or Swiss models?

3. How would increased participation by the federal government improve land use regulation in the United States? What concerns would this raise? Can a model that emphasizes local autonomy meet the demands of an increasingly national society?

4. For an interesting description of a non-Western land use system, see Mark T. Kremzner, *Managing Urban Land in China: The Emerging Legal Framework and its Role in Development,* 7 Pac. Rim L. & Pol'y J. 611 (1998).

C. THE GLOBALIZATION OF LAND USE REGULATION

International law has increasingly become a source of land use regulation. While land use issues were traditionally viewed as matters of domestic jurisdiction, transboundary impacts have led to greater international concern and, accordingly, greater involvement. International land use law has expanded rapidly to address a number of issues, such as those dealing with resource allocation, environmental impacts, human rights, and economic stability. Concerns particularly arise when a land use activity in one nation harms a neighboring nation or the international commons.

Daniel B. Magraw
International Land–Use Law

87 Am. Soc'y Int'l L. Proc. 488, 490–92 (1993)

[S]cores of international instruments exist that regulate land and land use, broadly defined. There is a vast diversity among these instruments. The large majority of them date from after World War II, but some antedate that. In terms of geographic coverage, the regimes range from global to regional to bilateral. . . .

- Regarding soil: the 1981 Food and Agriculture Organization (FAO) World Soil Charter;

- Regarding desertification: the 1984 Third Lome Convention (Pt. Two, Title I, ch. 2);

- Regarding forests: the 1983 International Tropical Timber Agreement;

- Regarding wetlands: the 1971 Ramsar Convention on Wetlands of International Importance Especially as Wildlife Habitat;

- Regarding wildlife: the 1973 Convention on the International Trade in Endangered Species (CITES);

- Regarding parklands: the 1972 Convention for the Protection of the World Cultural and Natural Heritage;

- Regarding agriculture: the 1988 FAO Guidelines on Flood Plain Management;

- Regarding mining: the 1986 United Nations Environment Programme (UNEP) Environmental Guidelines on Rehabilitation and Restoration of Land and Soil after Mining Activities. . . .

Several trends in international land law are identifiable. The first, and in some ways the most profound, is ecosystem management (also called ecosystem protection). Ecosystem management reflects the realization that the components of an ecosystem are interdependent, and thus that the best approach to environmental protection and conservation issues is one that involves examination and management of the entire relevant ecosystem. At the macro level (at least globally), this reflects the relatively recent recognition that the biosphere—that is, the concentric layers of land, water and air that sustain life—is a fragile system of interdependent elements. The 1992 Convention on Biological Diversity is based on an ecosystem management approach.

Ecosystem management does not admit of narrow, compartmentalized approaches to environmental protection. Analyzing and discussing land-use law involves an extremely broad array of issues, because land regulation and protection cannot be meaningfully separated from other environmental protection issues, such as migratory species protection, air pollution, waste disposal and pesticide use. Moreover, ecosystem management requires that ecosystems that straddle national frontiers be managed with reference to all the systems' components, regardless of where they are located.

Another trend in international land law is joint management of transboundary resources. This obviously is related to ecosystem management, but it is not as prevalent. A pioneering example is the joint United States–Canada High Ross Dam program, which involves the cooperation of many entities in both countries at all governmental levels. Another example, though less extensive, is the United States–Canada cooperation regarding Glacier National Park and Waterton Lakes National Park (which together were designated an "International Peace Park" by the two countries) under the United Nations Man and the Biosphere (MAB) Programme. Other examples include the nascent efforts of Colombia and Venezuela with respect to their transboundary river basins.

A third trend is designation of protected areas and special area management. The latter has primarily been used for marine resources, but the 1991 Antarctic Protocol on Environmental Protection embodies this approach. An interesting proposal, designed partly to avert international tension due to a boundary dispute, is an international park that would encompass the disputed boundary between Nepal and China. The theory is that creating the park would eliminate the need to demarcate that international boundary, thus converting controversy into cooperation.

Another trend, still in its infancy, is the integration of affected populations into the land regulatory regime. For example, the 1988 United States–Mexico Agreement on National Parks includes in its objectives "when possible[,] recognition of sustainable development alternatives for rural mexican [sic] communities located in those areas [and] the exploration of strategies for related cooperation with rural communities. . . ."

This trend reflects equitable considerations, as well as the practical fact that local populations, especially indigenous peoples with no other source of livelihood, are more useful as collaborators than as opponents to land protection. It may also reflect the realization that land-use rules have implications for land tenure, because there is some rough tie between ownership/occupancy of land, on the one hand, and the perceived legitimacy and economic value of the activity for which the land is used, on the other. This relationship can have devastating effects on individuals because of dislocation and cultural incompatibilities; the experience of the Ik in Africa is a particularly disheartening example of this.

Another extremely important trend—here, as in other areas of international environmental law—is special regard for the needs and situations of developing countries. The goal must be to treat them equitably, while at the same time recognizing their responsibilities as members of the international community and ensuring their effective participation in the relevant regimes.

The final trend I will mention is internationalization. It is commonly recognized that, as a general matter, international law and institutions affect ever more activities and intervene more and more deeply into societies. . . .

The phenomenon brings with it a special tension, however, in the context of land and land use. This tension is not just between the international community and nation-states, but also between the international community and individuals. It is generally appreciated that international instruments by themselves are meaningless; what is important is how an instrument is implemented and given effect through state behavior and, frequently, through behavior of individuals within states. Land is one of the most local of things; individuals feel a strong psychological tie to it. They must feel part of the relevant regime for that regime to achieve its goals. It is often the case that the local population, particularly the landowners, have the largest or most immediate stake in ensuring that land is used sustainably. And a significant argument exists that those persons have the right to a voice in decisions about how land is used. There is a real tension, therefore, between the need for an overarching regime that protects the land (and thus the biosphere), on the one hand, and the need for local support for, and local participation in forming, such a regime, on the other.

Notes

1.   What makes a seemingly local land use issue a matter of international concern? When should a nation's control of land use policies be supplanted by international law?

2.   Are there limits to using international law to resolve land use issues? What are the advantages and disadvantages of creating an international legal infrastructure for dealing with transboundary concerns? This subject is discussed in more detail in Chapter 15.

3.   Preservation of historic structures is a goal of many land use systems. Protection of a community's historic and cultural heritage enhances the identity of the community, and leads to increased stability and an enhanced sense of connection with others. However, historic structures can embody values and interests that transcend national boundaries and take on international significance. As the recent destruction of the Buddhist shrine in Bamiyan, Afghanistan demonstrates, historic preservation can be a matter of global concern. What role should the international community have in preserving historic structures?

4.   The transition to a market economy by many countries in Eastern Europe has reduced their ability to preserve historic and cultural monuments and buildings. Can privatization provide the incentives needed to safeguard such structures? Does the international community have a duty to protect these structures? For an article that explores this area, see Kirby Mitchell, *Rescuing Prague's Past: A Survey of Legislative Attempts at Architectural and Historical Preservation in Prague, Czech Republic*, 24 Ga. J. Int'l & Comp. L. 523 (1995).

Chapter 15

NUISANCE LAW

Nuisances do not respect national boundaries. Air and water pollution, groundwater contamination, and even nuclear fallout can cross borders freely. When activities within one nation cause damage to those outside its borders, the question of responsibility arises. In the common law system, nuisance law is based on the Latin maxim *sic utere tuo ut alienum non laedas*, meaning "use your own property in such a manner that you do not injure the property of another." Should this maxim become international law?

Problems arise when nuisance-like conduct in Nation A harms the citizens of Nation B. Nation A may be unwilling to impose costly regulations on its own industries, especially if the benefits of such regulations will fall to outsiders. The injured individuals in Nation B may not be able to gain jurisdiction over the culpable parties in Nation A, or may have difficulty enforcing any ruling they obtain. While transboundary nuisance problems have increasingly become the focus of international agreements, most of these instruments merely encourage the sharing of information or provide for consultation, rather than establishing firm rules of fault and liability.

The *Trail Smelter* arbitration is perhaps the most influential decision about transboundary pollution. It has helped to develop the customary international law that governs transboundary nuisances around the world.

TRAIL SMELTER ARBITRATION
(UNITED STATES v. CANADA)
Ad Hoc International Arbitral Tribunal
3 U.N. Rep. Int'l Awards 1911, 1938–43, 1945, 1963–66 (1941)

HOSTIE, WARREN and GREENSHIELDS, ARBITRATORS.

This Tribunal is constituted under, and its powers are derived from and limited by, the Convention between the United States of

America and the Dominion of Canada signed at Ottawa, April 15, 1935....

The controversy is between two Governments involving damage occurring, or having occurred, in the territory of one of them (the United States of America) and alleged to be due to an agency situated in the territory of the other (the Dominion of Canada). In this controversy, the Tribunal did not sit and is not sitting to pass upon claims presented by individuals or on behalf of one or more individuals by their Government, although individuals may come within the meaning of "parties concerned."...

As between the two countries involved, each has an equal interest that if a nuisance is proved, the indemnity to damaged parties for proven damage shall be just and adequate and each has also an equal interest that unproven or unwarranted claims shall not be allowed. For, while the United States' interests may now be claimed to be injured by the operations of a Canadian corporation, it is equally possible that at some time in the future Canadian interests might be claimed to be injured by an American corporation....

The duty imposed upon the Tribunal by the Convention was to "finally decide" the following questions:

(1) Whether damage caused by the Trail Smelter in the State of Washington has occurred since the first day of January, 1932, and, if so, what indemnity should be paid therefore?

(2) In the event of the answer to the first part of the preceding question being in the affirmative, whether the Trail Smelter should be required to refrain from causing damage in the State of Washington in the future and, if so, to what extent?

(3) In the light of the answer to the preceding question, what measures or regime, if any, should be adopted or maintained by the Trail Smelter?

(4) What indemnity or compensation, if any, should be paid on account of any decision or decisions rendered by the Tribunal pursuant to the next two preceding questions?

Concerning Question No. 1, in the statement presented by the Agent for the Government of the United States, claims for damages of $1,849,156.16 with interest of $250,855.01—total $2,100,011.17—were presented, divided into seven categories, in respect of (a) cleared land and improvements; (b) of uncleared land and improvements; (c) live stock; (d) property in the town of Northport; (e) wrong done the United States in violation of sovereignty, measured by cost of investigation from January 1, 1932, to

June 30, 1936; (f) interest on $350,000 accepted in satisfaction of damage to January 1, 1932, but not paid on that date; (g) business enterprises. The area claimed to be damaged contained "more than 140,000 acres," including the town of Northport.

The Tribunal disallowed the claims of the United States with reference to items (c), (d), (e), (f) and (g) but allowed them, in part, with respect to the remaining items (a) and (b).

In conclusion...the Tribunal answered Question No. 1 as follows:

> Damage caused by the Trail Smelter in the State of Washington has occurred since the first day of January, 1932, and up to October 1, 1937, and the indemnity to be paid therefore is seventy-eight thousand dollars ($78,000), and is to be complete and final indemnity and compensation for all damage which occurred between such dates. Interest at the rate of six per centum per year will be allowed on the above sum of seventy-eight thousand dollars ($78,000) from the date of the filing of this report and decision until date of payment. This decision is not subject to alteration or modification by the Tribunal hereafter. The fact of existence of damage, if any, occurring after October 1, 1937, and the indemnity to be paid therefore, if any, the Tribunal will determine in its final decision.

Answering Questions No. 2 and No. 3, the Tribunal decided that, until a final decision should be made, the Trail Smelter should be subject to a temporary regime (described more in detail in Part Four of the present decision) and a trial period was established to a date not later than October 1, 1940, in order to enable the Tribunal to establish a permanent regime based on a "more adequate and intensive study", since the Tribunal felt that the information that had been placed before it did not enable it to determine at that time with sufficient certainty upon a permanent regime....

The Columbia River has its source in the Dominion of Canada. At a place in British Columbia named Trail, it flows past a smelter located in a gorge, where zinc and lead are smelted in large quantities. From Trail, its course is easterly and then it swings in a long curve to the international boundary line, at which point it is running in a southwesterly direction; and its course south of the boundary continues in that general direction. The distance from Trail to the boundary line is about seven miles as the crow flies or about eleven miles, following the course of the river (and possibly a slightly shorter distance by following the contour of the valley)....

The town of Northport is located on the east bank of the river, about nineteen miles from Trail by the river, and about thirteen miles as the crow flies. It is to be noted that mountains extending more or less in an easterly and westerly direction rise to the south between Trail and the boundary. . . .

The direction of the surface wind is, in general, from the northeast down the river valley, but this varies at different times of day and in different seasons. . . .

In 1896, a smelter was started under American auspices near the locality known as Trail, B.C. In 1906, the Consolidated Mining and Smelting Company of Canada, Limited, obtained a charter of incorporation from the Canadian authorities, and that company acquired the smelter plant at Trail as it then existed. Since that time, the Canadian company, without interruption, has operated the Smelter, and from time to time has greatly added to the plant until it has become one of the best and largest equipped smelting plants on the American continent. In 1925 and 1927, two stacks of the plant were erected to 409 feet in height and the Smelter greatly increased its daily smelting of zinc and lead ores. This increased production resulted in more sulphur dioxide fumes and higher concentrations being emitted into the air. In 1916, about 5,000 tons of sulphur per month were emitted; in 1924, about 4,700 tons; in 1926, about 9,000 tons—an amount which rose near to 10,000 tons per month in 1930. In other words, about 300–350 tons of sulphur were being emitted daily in 1930. . . .

From 1925, at least, to 1937, damage occurred in the State of Washington, resulting from the sulphur dioxide emitted from the Trail Smelter. . . .

The first problem which arises is whether the question should be answered on the basis of the law followed in the United States or on the basis of international law. The Tribunal, however, finds that this problem need not be solved here as the law followed in the United States in dealing with the quasi-sovereign rights of the States of the Union, in the matter of air pollution, whilst more definite, is in conformity with the general rules of international law. . . .

As Professor Eagleton puts it (*Responsibility of States in International Law*, 1928, p. 80): "A State owes at all times a duty to protect other States against injurious acts by individuals from within its jurisdiction." A great number of such general pronouncements by leading authorities concerning the duty of a State to respect other States and their territory have been presented to the Tribunal. These and many others have been carefully examined. International decisions, in various matters, from the Alabama case onward, and also earlier ones, are based on the same general principle, and, indeed, this principle, as such, has not been questioned by Canada. But the real difficulty often arises rather when it comes to determine what, *pro subjecta materie*, is deemed to constitute an injurious act.

A case concerning, as the present one does, territorial relations, decided by the Federal Court of Switzerland between the Cantons of Soleure and Argovia, may serve to illustrate the relativity of the rule. Soleure brought a suit against her sister State to enjoin use of a shooting establishment which endangered her territory. The court, in granting the injunction, said: "This right (sovereignty) excludes...not only the usurpation and exercise of sovereign rights (of another State)...but also an actual encroachment which might prejudice the natural use of the territory and the free movement of its inhabitants." As a result of the decision, Argovia made plans for the improvement of the existing installations. These, however, were considered as insufficient protection by Soleure. The Canton of Argovia then moved the Federal Court to decree that the shooting be again permitted after completion of the projected improvements. This motion was granted. "The demand of the Government of Soleure," said the court, "that all endangerment be absolutely abolished apparently goes too far." The court found that all risk whatever had not been eliminated, as the region was flat and absolutely safe shooting ranges were only found in mountain valleys; that there was a federal duty for the communes to provide facilities for military target practice and that "no more precautions may be demanded for shooting ranges near the boundaries of two Cantons than are required for shooting ranges in the interior of a Canton." R.O. 26 I, p. 450, 451; R.O. 41, I, p. 137; see D. Schindler, "The Administration of Justice in the Swiss Federal Court in Intercantonal Disputes," *American Journal of International Law*, Vol. 15 (1921), pp. 172–174.

No case of air pollution dealt with by an international tribunal has been brought to the attention of the Tribunal nor does the Tribunal know of any such case. The nearest analogy is that of water pollution. But, here also, no decision of an international tribunal has been cited or has been found.

There are, however, as regards both air pollution and water pollution, certain decisions of the Supreme Court of the United States which may legitimately be taken as a guide in this field of international law, for it is reasonable to follow by analogy, in international cases, precedents established by that court in dealing with controversies between States of the Union or with other controversies concerning the quasi-sovereign rights of such States, where no contrary rule prevails in international law and no reason for rejecting such precedents can be adduced from the limitations of sovereignty inherent in the Constitution of the United States.

In the suit of the *State of Missouri v. the State of Illinois* (200 U.S. 496, 521) concerning the pollution, within the boundaries of Illinois, of the Illinois River, an affluent of the Mississippi flowing into the latter where it forms the boundary between that State and Missouri, an injunction was refused. "Before this court ought to intervene", said the court, "the case should be of serious magnitude, clearly and fully proved, and the principle to be applied should be one which the court is prepared deliberately to maintain against all considerations on the other side. (See *Kansas v. Colorado*, 185 U.S. 125.)" The court found that the practice complained of was general along the shores of the Mississippi River at the time, that it was followed by Missouri itself and that thus a standard was set up by the defendant which the claimant was entitled to invoke....

In the matter of air pollution itself, the leading decisions are those of the Supreme Court in the *State of Georgia v. Tennessee Copper Company and Ducktown Sulphur, Copper and Iron Company, Limited.* Although dealing with a suit against private companies, the decisions were on questions cognate to those here at issue. Georgia stated that it had in vain sought relief from the State of Tennessee, on whose territory the smelters were located, and the court defined the nature of the suit by saying: "This is a suit by a State for an injury to it in its capacity of quasi-sovereign. In that capacity, the State has an interest independent of and behind the titles of its citizens, in all the earth and air within its domain."

The Tribunal, therefore, finds that the above decisions, taken as a whole, constitute an adequate basis for its conclusions, namely, that, under the principles of international law, as well as of the law of the United States, no State has the right to use or permit the use of its territory in such a manner as to cause injury by fumes in or to the territory of another or the properties or persons therein, when the case is of serious consequence and the injury is established by clear and convincing evidence....

Considering the circumstances of the case, the Tribunal holds that the Dominion of Canada is responsible in international law for the conduct of the Trail Smelter. Apart from the undertakings in the Convention, it is, therefore, the duty of the Government of the Dominion of Canada to see to it that this conduct should be in conformity with the obligation of the Dominion under international law as herein determined.

The Tribunal, therefore, answers Question No. 2 as follows: (2) So long as the present conditions in the Columbia River Valley prevail, the Trail Smelter shall be required to refrain from causing any damage through fumes in the State of Washington; the damage herein referred to and its extent being such as would be recoverable under the decisions of the courts of the United States in suits between private individuals. The indemnity for such damage should be fixed in such manner as the Governments, acting under Article XI of the Convention, should agree upon. . . .

[A]nd since the Tribunal is of the opinion that damage may occur in the future unless the operations of the Smelter shall be subject to some control, in order to avoid damage occurring, the Tribunal now decides that a regime or measure of control shall be applied to the operations of the Smelter and shall remain in full force unless and until modified in accordance with the provisions hereinafter set forth. . . .

Notes

1. This dispute arose over sulphur dioxide fumes emitted by a smelter in Trail, Canada, that were carried by prevailing winds down the Columbia River Valley into the United States. Initially, Canada and the United States agreed to refer the issue to the International Joint Commission (IJC) for resolution. The IJC had been established by the Boundary Waters Treaty of 1909 between Canada and the United States. In considering the dispute, the IJC found that the smelter had caused $350,000 in damage through 1931. The IJC's report produced further negotiations, resulting in a convention that led to the arbitration.

2. What duty should a source nation owe an affected nation regarding transboundary nuisance effects? The *Trail Smelter* panel implied that there should be "strict liability" for "serious consequences" that are proven by "clear and convincing evidence." Do you agree that such standards are appropriate?

3. Why should Canada be responsible for the conduct of the Trail smelter? Is it responsible for all activities of its citizens that have transboundary effects? Should a nation be responsible only for transboundary injuries caused by its own actions or those of its agents?

4. Should international law limit actions for transboundary effects to situations that involve damage to private property, as opposed to mere interference with its use and enjoyment? What would be the basis for such a distinction?

5. In his excellent essay, *Golden Rules for Transboundary Pollution*, 46 Duke L.J. 931 (1997), Thomas Merrill suggests a new approach for resolving disputes about transboundary pollution. Applying what he calls "golden norms," Professor Merrill reasons that the "source state should treat the affected state the way it treats its own citizens, and the affected state should demand of the source state no more than it demands of its own citizens." *Id.* at 1018. Is Professor Merrill's approach workable?

6. The *Trail Smelter* panel cited past decisions of the United States Supreme Court as authority for its ruling. Should decisions of the Court provide authority for dealing with transboundary issues? Why?

7. For more detailed analysis of *Trail Smelter*, see generally Alexandre Kiss & Dinah Shelton, International Environmental Law 107 (1991) and Alfred Rubin, *Pollution by Analogy: The Trail Smelter Arbitration*, 50 Or. L. Rev. 259 (1971).

Chapter 16

TAKINGS

A. PHYSICAL EXPROPRIATION

Does international law regulate the ability of a nation to expropriate private property within its borders? For example, suppose that Smith, a citizen of Nation A, buys a factory in Nation B; Nation B physically seizes possession of the factory and uses it for government purposes. Must Nation B now compensate Smith for her loss?

Until the mid-twentieth century, the answer to this question was almost certainly "yes." The investor-oriented nations of Europe and North America, who had the most influence on the development of international law principles in the era, agreed that one nation could not take the property of a citizen of another nation without compensation. A series of international arbitrations and other decisions applied this rule in expropriation disputes. Arguably, it became a "customary principle" of international law. However, after World War II, as developing nations gained independence—and challenged the conventional rule—this international consensus began to erode.

BANCO NACIONAL DE CUBA v. CHASE MANHATTAN BANK

United States Court of Appeals for the Second Circuit
658 F.2d 875, 888–91 (1981)

KEARSE, J.

[In 1960, the Republic of Cuba expropriated the four Cuban branches of Chase Manhattan Bank ("Chase"). These assets were transferred to Banco Nacional de Cuba, which became wholly owned and operated by the Cuban government. Banco Nacional later sued Chase in the United States on other claims. In that action, Chase asserted a counterclaim seeking damages for the expropriation of its Cuban branches. The district court found for Chase on the counterclaim in an amount exceeding $6,900,000. In resolving the appeal filed by Banco Nacional, the Second Circuit discussed the international law principles governing expropriation.]

...The view long held by the United States is that an alien whose property is expropriated is entitled to "prompt, adequate, and effective" compensation. Described some two decades ago as the "orthodox position,"...this view has been known as the "Hull Doctrine" since its most celebrated expression in a communication from former United States Secretary of State Cordell Hull to the government of Mexico in 1938 on the subject of the Mexican agrarian takings. ...

There has been some international support for the Hull Doctrine.... And the view that international law requires full compensation was adopted as recently as 1965 by the Restatement [of Foreign Relations Law of the United States].

As recognized by the Restatement, however, there have been contrary views, some moderate and some extreme, as to the compensation obligations of expropriating states.... [S]ome nations have taken a position at the very opposite end of the spectrum from the Hull Doctrine, arguing that an expropriating nation need pay the alien no compensation whatever. The Restatement Reporters' Notes observe, for example, that on occasion some Latin American states "have insisted specifically that international law imposes no duty to pay compensation when property is taken pursuant to a general program of social or economic reform." ... And the Supreme Court in *Sabbatino* observed as follows:

...Certain representatives of the newly independent and underdeveloped countries have questioned whether rules of state responsibility toward aliens can bind nations that have not consented to them and it is argued that the traditionally articulated standards governing expropriation of property reflect "imperialist" interests and are inappropriate to the circumstances of emergent states. ...

Finally, actions taken by the General Assembly of the United Nations on this subject..., while they do not have the force of law ... are of considerable interest. ... [I]n 1974, the General Assembly adopted Resolution 3281 (XXIX), which revived the concept of "appropriate compensation," but stated that it "should" be paid rather than it "shall" be paid, and made no reference to international law. Article 2 [of the Resolution, the "Charter of Economic Duties and Rights of States"] stated in part as follows:

2. Each State has the right:

(c) To nationalize, expropriate or transfer ownership of foreign property, in which case appropriate compensation should be paid by the State adopting such measures, taking into account its relevant laws and regulations and all circumstances that the State considers pertinent. . . .

The United States, with thirteen other states, proposed an amendment to Article 2, declaring that each state has the right to "nationalize, expropriate or requisition foreign property for a public purpose, provided that just compensation in light of all relevant circumstances shall be paid." . . . This amendment was rejected, and the United States voted against Resolution 3281 (XXIX). The final vote was 120, including Cuba, for and 6 against, with 10 abstentions.

This overview of the actions of the members of the General Assembly presents at best a confused and confusing picture as to what the consensus may be as to the responsibilities of an expropriating nation to pay "appropriate compensation," and just what that term may mean. The resolutions, the views of commentators, and the positions taken by individual states or blocs are varied, diverse, and not easily reconciled. The reporters for a revision of the Restatement currently in the drafting stage have summed it up well: "It is difficult. . . to state in black or even gray letter what is the international law now as regards compensation for expropriated alien properties." . . .

[W]e reject the position espoused by some states that property may be expropriated without an obligation on the part of the nationalizing state to pay any compensation therefor. Whether or not an expropriation violates international law and we note that the present expropriations have been held unlawful, and that ruling is not here contested we believe that the prevalent view is the traditional view, to wit, that the failure to pay any compensation to the victim of an expropriation constitutes a violation of international law. . . .

Note

In light of the 1974 U.N. General Assembly resolution and other developments, many investor nations concluded that they could not rely on traditional international law to protect foreign investments from expropriation. As a result, they began to seek such protection through the treaty process. Over 2,200 bilateral investment treaties have now been adopted; these are treaties that govern the investments that the citizens of one nation make inside another nation. Most of these agreements contain expropriation provisions that incorporate the Hull Doctrine or parallel language. A number of regional investment treaties—including the North American Free Trade Agreement discussed below—contain similar protections. Some scholars suggest that this network of treaties can be seen as reflecting a norm of customary international law: a country that seizes the property of a foreign national must pay just compensation.

B.   REGULATORY TAKINGS

We now turn to a second question: does international law protect against regulatory takings? Suppose again that Smith, a citizen of Nation A, buys a factory in Nation B, fully complying with all laws. Nation B now adopts a new law that forces Smith to close the factory. Nation B has not physically expropriated Smith's property, but the effect on Smith is the same: Smith loses the value of her investment. Must Nation B compensate Smith? Would it make a difference if Smith were instead a citizen of Nation B? We will consider these issues both under the North American Free Trade Agreement ("NAFTA") and the Convention for the Protection of Human Rights and Fundamental Freedoms.

NAFTA was adopted in 1992 to establish a free trade area among Canada, Mexico, and the United States. It seeks to eliminate trade barriers, promote fair competition, and expand investment opportunities in the territories of the parties. Chapter 11 is a key component of NAFTA; it encourages foreign investment by providing protection against expropriation and similar actions. Thus, as set forth below, Article 1110 prohibits (1) direct expropriation, (2) indirect expropriation, and (3) "measures tantamount to ... expropriation." This language was interpreted by an international arbitration panel in *Metalclad Corporation v. United Mexican States*, which is excerpted below.

NORTH AMERICAN FREE TRADE AGREEMENT

(1994)

Article 201: For the purposes of this Agreement, unless otherwise specified: ... *[M]easure* includes any law, regulation, procedure, requirement or practice; ...

Article 1110: Expropriation and Compensation

1.   No Party may directly or indirectly nationalize or expropriate an investment of an investor of another Party in its territory or take a measure tantamount to nationalization or expropriation of such an investment ("expropriation"), except:

(a) for a public purpose;

(b) on a non-discriminatory basis;

(c) in accordance with due process of law ...; and

(d) on payment of compensation in accordance with paragraphs 2 through 6 [which require prompt payment of "the fair market value of the expropriated investment"]

Article 1114: Environmental Measures

1. Nothing in this Chapter shall be construed to prevent a Party from adopting, maintaining or enforcing any measure otherwise consistent with this Chapter that it considers appropriate to ensure that investment activity in its territory is undertaken in a manner sensitive to environmental concerns. . . .

Article 1139: Definitions

For the purposes of this Chapter: . . .*investment* means: (a) an enterprise; . . . (g) real estate or other property, tangible or intangible, acquired in the expectation or used for the purpose of economic benefit or other business purposes; and (h) interests arising from the commitment of capital or other resources in the territory of a Party to economic activity in such territory. . . .

METALCLAD CORPORATION v. UNITED MEXICAN STATES

International Centre for the Settlement of Investment Disputes
Case No. Arb(AF)/97/1 (2000), 40 I.L.M. 36, 37, 50–51, 54 (2001)

LAUTERPACHT, CIVILETTI, and SIQUEIROS, ARBITRATORS.

1. This dispute arises out of the activities of the Claimant, Metalclad Corporation, in the Mexican Municipality of Guadalcazar (hereinafter "Guadalcazar"), located in the Mexican State of San Luis Potosi (hereinafter "SLP"). Metalclad alleges that Respondent, the United Mexican States (hereinafter "Mexico"), through its local governments of SLP and Guadalcazar, interfered with its development and operation of a hazardous waste landfill. Metalclad claims that this interference is a violation of the Chapter Eleven investment provisions of the North American Free Trade Agreement (hereinafter "NAFTA"). . . .

[A Mexican company, Confinamiento Tecnico de Residuos Industriales ("COTERIN"), owned title to a 2,000–acre tract of remote land located within Guadalcazar (which is akin to a county in the United States). In 1991, COTERIN applied to Guadalcazar for a permit to build a hazardous waste landfill on the site, but the application was refused. COTERIN then received permits from the federal government of Mexico to construct and operate such a landfill on the property; and the state of SLP granted a state land use permit to construct the landfill. In 1993, Metalclad, a Delaware corporation, entered into an option agreement to purchase COTERIN. One condition of the option agreement was either that (1) the municipal permit be issued or (2) COTERIN secure a judgment from the Mexican courts that a municipal permit was unnecessary. However, after Mexican federal officials assured Metalclad that a municipal permit was not required, Metalclad waived this condition and completed the purchase.

Metalclad began construction of the landfill in May, 1994. In October, 1994, Guadalcazar ordered that all construction cease, because a municipal permit had not been issued. Metalclad was told by federal officials that it should apply for the permit "to facilitate an amicable relationship" with Guadalcazar and that the permit would be issued as a matter of course. In November, 1994, Metalclad resumed construction and applied for the municipal permit. Construction was completed in March, 1995. Local residents protested at the "open house" that was held to celebrate the completion of the landfill, blocking the entry and exit of buses carrying guests and workers. In December, 1995, Guadalcazar denied Metalclad's application for the municipal permit; in January 1996, it persuaded a Mexican court to issue an injunction preventing Metalclad from operating the landfill. Negotiations to resolve the stalemate were unsuccessful. The landfill never opened and never operated. Metalclad then brought an arbitration proceeding under NAFTA against the federal Mexican government. In September, 1997, three days before his term of office ended, the Governor of SLP issued an Ecological Decree that designated a huge region—including the landfill site—as a preserve for the protection of rare cacti. This Decree effectively prevented operation of the landfill.]

102. NAFTA Article 1110 provides that "[n]o party shall directly or indirectly...expropriate an investment...or take a measure tantamount to...expropriation...except: (a) for a public purpose; (b) on a non-discriminatory basis; (c) in accordance with due process of law...; and (d) on payment of compensation..." "A measure" is defined in Article 201(1) as including "any law, regulation, procedure, requirement or practice."

103. Thus, expropriation under NAFTA includes not only open, deliberate and acknowledged takings of property, such as outright seizure or formal or obligatory transfer of title in favour of the host State, but also covert or incidental interference with the use of property which has the effect of depriving the owner, in whole or in significant part, of the use or reasonably-to-be-expected economic benefit of property even if not necessarily to the obvious benefit of the host State.

104. By permitting or tolerating the conduct of Guadalcazar in relation to Metalclad which the Tribunal has already held amounts to unfair and inequitable treatment...and by thus participating or acquiescing in the denial to Metalclad of the right to operate the landfill, notwithstanding the fact that that the project was fully

approved and endorsed by the federal government, Mexico must be held to have taken a measure tantamount to expropriation in violation of NAFTA Article 1110(1).

105. The Tribunal holds that the exclusive authority for siting and permitting a hazardous waste landfill resides with the Mexican federal government. . . .

106. As determined earlier. . ., the Municipality denied the local construction permit in part because of the Municipality's perception of the adverse environmental effects of the hazardous waste landfill and the geological unsuitability of the landfill site. In so doing, the Municipality acted outside its authority. As stated above, the Municipality's denial of the construction permit without any basis in the proposed physical construction or any defect in the site, and extended by its subsequent administrative and judicial actions. . .effectively and unlawfully prevented the Claimant's operation of the landfill.

107. These measures, taken together with the representations of the Mexican federal government, on which Metalclad relied, and the absence of a timely, orderly or substantive basis for the denial by the Municipality of the local construction permit, amount to an indirect expropriation. . . .

109. Although not strictly necessary for its conclusion, the Tribunal also identifies as a further ground for a finding of expropriation the Ecological Decree issued by the Governor of SLP on September 20, 1997. This Decree covers an area of 188,758 hectares [over 700 square miles] within the "Real de Guadalcazar" that includes the landfill site, and created therein an ecological preserve. This Decree had the effect of barring forever the operation of the landfill. . . .

111. The Tribunal need not decide or consider the motivation or intent of the adoption of the Ecological Decree. Indeed, a finding of expropriation on the basis of the Ecological Decree is not essential to the Tribunal's finding of a violation of NAFTA Article 1110. However, the Tribunal considers that the implementation of the Ecological Decree would, in and of itself, constitute an act tantamount to expropriation.

112. In conclusion, the Tribunal holds that Mexico has indirectly expropriated Metalclad's investment without providing compensation to Metalclad for the expropriation. Mexico has violated Article 1110 of the NAFTA. . . .

131. For the reasons stated above, the Tribunal hereby decides that. . .the Respondent shall. . .pay to Metalclad the amount of $16,685,000.00.

Notes

1. What were the specific governmental acts that constituted an indirect expropriation, according to the tribunal? Would a prudent investor begin construction of a project even though the local government has not yet granted a building permit?

2. The federal Mexican government later brought suit in British Columbia—the site of the underlying arbitration—to challenge the *Metalclad* decision. The British Columbia Supreme Court held that the Ecological Decree was an illegal expropriation under Article 1110; but it rejected the other Article 1110 claims that Metalclad raised. See *United Mexican States v. Metalclad Corp.*, [2001] 89 B.C.L.R.3d 359.

3. NAFTA Article 1114 permits a party to ensure that any investment activity within its territory is "undertaken in a manner sensitive to environmental concerns." Here, the Governor of San Luis Potosi determined that the project site should be part of a preserve for rare cacti. Why didn't Article 1114 shield Mexico from liability for expropriation? To what extent does NAFTA interfere with a nation's ability to preserve the natural environment?

4. How broad is the tribunal's test? At Paragraph 103, the decision extends the reach of Section 1110 to "covert or incidental interference with the use of property which has the effect of depriving the owner, in whole or in significant part, of the use or reasonably-to-be-expected economic benefit of property." Suppose a U.S. corporation purchases 100 acres of land in Mexico, with the goal of building a subdivision of vacation homes, which is a use permitted at the time by Mexican law. If the Mexican state government later declares that half of the land is environmentally sensitive and, accordingly, must remain in its natural condition, would this be an expropriation under the *Metalclad* approach?

5. Does *Metalclad* provide more protection against regulatory takings than would be available under domestic law in the United States? *See* Vicki Been & Joel Beauvais, *The Global Fifth Amendment? NAFTA's Investment Protection and the Misguided Quest for an International "Regulatory Takings" Doctrine*, 78 N.Y.U. L. Rev. 30 (2003). If so, what are the implications of this difference?

FREDIN v. SWEDEN

European Court of Human Rights
13 Eur. H.R. Rep. 784, 786, 790–96, 800 (1991)

RYSSDAL, VILHJÁLMSSON, PETTITI, WALSH, MACDONALD, RUSSO, DE MEYER, MARTENS, and PALM, JUDGES.

. . .

8. Mr. Anders Fredin, an agricultural engineer, and his wife Mrs. Maria Fredin [both citizens of Sweden] own several parcels of land in the municipality of Botkyrka [in Sweden]. On the land there is a

farm and a gravel pit. The parcel where the gravel pit is located consists of 27 hectares [about 65 acres] and is called Ström 1:3. It was specifically created in 1969 from parts of the other properties with a view to the exploitation of the pit. . . .

[Sweden adopted an Act that prohibited the extraction of gravel without a permit. Mr. Fredin's parents, who then owned the property, obtained the necessary permit in 1963, which provided for gravel excavation to be carried out through 1993; the permit required that the operators reshape and restore the land after mining ended. A 1973 amendment to the Act empowered the County Administrative Board to revoke permits that were more than 10 years old, in order to protect the environment. The parents conveyed title to Anders and Maria Fredin in 1977. In the early 1980s, the Fredins invested approximately 2,250,000 kronor (over $400,000) in the gravel excavation business. In 1983, the Board approved the transfer of the permit to the Fredins, but notified them that it was considering amending the permit to require that gravel extraction end in 1984 because continued mining was damaging the environment. In 1984, the Board ordered that the extraction of gravel should cease by the end of 1987. The Fredins appealed this decision through the Swedish court system, claiming that they had a protected right to mine gravel through 1993, but lost. If the permit had extended through 1993, the gravel pit would be worth approximately 15,500,000 kronor (over $2,000,000); without the permit, the gravel pit was worth less than 1,000 kronor (about $125). Thus, the revocation of the permit took more than 99.99% of the land's value. The Fredins asserted that this was the "only case in Sweden in which the authorities had stopped an ongoing gravel exploitation business...." Before the European Court of Human Rights, the Fredins argued that the revocation of the permit violated their right to property under Article 1 of Protocol 1 to the Convention for the Protection of Human Rights and Fundamental Freedoms, which is reprinted in Chapter 2.]

33. According to section 1 of the Act, everyone must show respect and circumspection in his or her dealings with nature. In addition, all necessary measures have to be taken to limit or counteract any damage to nature which is bound to result from any works undertaken or otherwise. . . .

35. Section 18 of the Act prohibits, *inter alia*, extraction of gravel for purposes other than the domestic needs of the landowner without a permit from the County Administrative Board. The section also specifies that: . . . The permit shall be made subject to such conditions as are necessary to limit or counteract the harmful effects of the enterprise on the natural environment. . . .

41.   Article 1 [of Protocol 1 to the Convention] guarantees in substance the right of property. It consists of three distinct rules. The first, which is expressed in the first sentence of the first paragraph and is of a general nature, lays down the principle of peaceful enjoyment of property. The second rule, in the second sentence of the same paragraph, covers deprivation of possessions and subjects it to certain conditions. The third, contained in the second paragraph, recognizes that the Contracting States are entitled, amongst other things, to control the use of property in accordance with the general interest by enforcing such laws as they deem necessary for the purpose. . . .

42.   There was no formal expropriation of the applicants' property. However, for the purposes of Article 1 of Protocol No. 1 the concept of "deprivation" covers not only formal expropriation but also measures which amount to a *de facto* expropriation. . . . The applicants contended that they had been the victims of such a *de facto* deprivation of property, whereas the Government and the Commission considered the revocation of the permit to be a measure for the control of use of property. . . .

44.   The applicants have stressed that the revocation, taken with other existing regulatory measures, left no meaningful alternative use for Ström 1:3. They have also maintained that the revocation deprived the property of all its value.

45.   As to the first point, . . . the applicants' possibilities of using their possessions cannot be assessed by looking at Ström 1:3 in isolation. . . . In order to take into account the realities of the situation, the effects of the revocation have to be ascertained in the light also of the situation obtaining on the applicants' surrounding properties. Nothing indicates, however, that the revocation directly affected these other properties. Viewing the question from this perspective, the Court does not find it established that the revocation took away all meaningful use of the properties in question.

46.   With regard to the second argument, the Court first notes that the applicants are still the owners of the gravel resources on Ström 1:3. It recognizes nevertheless that the revocation of the 1963 permit did have serious adverse effects. . . One has, however, to bear in mind that, over the years, the exploitation of gravel has been more and more regulated and, in fact, restricted. . . . Thus, the amendment introduced on 1 July 1973 to the. . .Act empowered the authorities to revoke, without compensation, old permits, such as the applicants' after 10 years had passed, that is after 1 July 1983. As a consequence, the applicants' possibilities of continuing their gravel exploitation business after this date became uncertain.

47.   In light of the above considerations, the revocation of the applicants' permit to exploit gravel cannot be regarded as a depriva-

tion of possessions, within the meaning of the first paragraph of Article 1 of Protocol No. 1. It must be considered as a control of use of property falling within the scope of the second paragraph of the Article.

48. Applicants did not contest the legitimacy of the aim of the... Act, that is the protection of nature. The Court recognises for its part that in today's society the protection of the environment is an increasingly important consideration. . . .

51. It is well-established case law that...an interference [with rights safeguarded by the Convention] must achieve a "fair balance" between the demands of the general interest of the community and the requirements of the protection of the individual's fundamental rights. The search for balance is reflected in the structure of Article 1 as a whole, and therefore also in the second paragraph thereof: there must be a reasonable relationship of proportionality between the means employed and the aim pursued. In determining whether this requirement is met, the Court recognizes that the State enjoys a wide margin of appreciation with regard both to choosing the means of enforcement and to ascertaining whether the consequences of enforcement are justified in the general interest for the purpose of achieving the object of the law in question.

52. According to the applicants, the circumstances obtaining at the time they made their investments gave them legitimate reason to believe that they would be able to continue the exploitation of the gravel pit for a long time. They claimed that the revocation at short notice of their right to do so did not strike a fair balance between the individual and the general interests involved. . . .

54. The applicants initiated their investments seven years after the entry into force of the 1973 amendment to section 18 of the . . . Act which clearly provided for the potential revocation of existing permits after the expiry of the 10–year period that started to run on 1 July 1975. They must therefore reasonably have been aware of the possibility that they might lose their permit after 1 July 1983. In addition, it is clear that the authorities did not give them any assurances that they would be allowed to continue to extract gravel after this date. ...Accordingly, when embarking on their investments, the applicants could have relied only on the authorities' obligation, when taking decisions relating to nature conservation, to take due account of their interests, as prescribed by [the Act]. This obligation cannot, at the time the applicants made their investments, reasonably have founded any legitimate expectations on their part of being able to continue exploitation for a long period of time. . . .

55. Having regard to the foregoing and to the legitimate aim pursued by the...Act, the Court finds that it cannot be said the

revocation decision complained of by applicants was inappropriate or disproportionate. . . .

VILHJÁLMSSON, J. (concurring).

. . . Implementation measures in the field of nature conservation take many forms and will often have to continue for years. By their very nature, they may cause inconvenience to certain people since equal treatment of all persons in similar situations may not only be impractical but also impossible. It is for the Government of Sweden and not for our Court to say whether the aim of the nature conservation legislation should be realized by the closing of one or several gravel pits or if no measures should be taken. . . .

Notes

1. Is *Fredin* consistent with *Metalclad*? In both cases, a government decision not to permit a particular land use caused substantial harm to the owners; and in both cases, the owners were on notice of possible permit problems before they invested. If anything, shouldn't the Fredins have a stronger claim for compensation, since their gravel pit had been an operating business for many years, while the hazardous waste landfill owned by Metalclad Corporation was new? Or does this fact harm the Fredins' case?

2. Which activity poses the greater environmental threat—the gravel mine in *Fredin* or the hazardous waste landfill in *Metalclad*? Is this relevant?

3. If we view both *Fredin* and *Metalclad* as attempts to balance internationally-recognized property rights with domestic environmental concerns, which decision strikes the best balance? Why?

4. Compare the tests used in *Fredin* and *Metalclad*. Which test gives greater protection to property rights? What explains this difference?

5. Isn't it reasonable for landowners like the Fredins to assume that Sweden will consider the right to property in deciding whether to revoke a permit? What does Judge Vilhjálmsson mean when he states that it is "not for our Court to say" whether no pits, one pit, or several pits should be closed?

*

Index

References are to Pages

155

References are to Pages

†